Success by Design: How Smart Entrepreneurs and Creators Build Lasting Habits

Connie Ragen Green's Titles

- *In Pursuit of Healthy-Ness: How I Reinvented My Life with Intermittent Fasting*
- *Speakers! The Quick Public Speaking to Business Method™ - Turning Your Talk into an Ongoing Revenue Stream*
- *The Road Trip: An Entrepreneur's Journey of Self-Discovery*
- *Authors! The Quick Book to Business Method™ - Turning Your Book into an Ongoing Revenue Stream*
- *Local Business Marketing: Making the Phone Ring for Businesses*
- *Kids and Money – Teaching Financial Responsibility and Values to Children*
- *Rethinking the Work Ethic: Embrace the Struggle and Exceed Your Own Potential*
- *Book. Blog. Broadcast. The Trifecta of Entrepreneurial Success*
- *Write. Publish. Prosper. How to Write Prolifically, Publish Globally, and Prosper Eternally*
- *Living the Internet Lifestyle: Quit Your Job, Become an Entrepreneur, and Live Your Ideal Life*
- *The Weekend Marketer: Say Goodbye to the '9 to 5', Build an Online Business, and Live the Life You Love*
- *Huge Profits with a Tiny List: 50 Ways to Use Relationship Marketing to Increase Your Bottom Line*
- *Essays at the Intersection of Hope and Synchronicity*
- *Self-Directed: Inspire, Motivate, and Empower Yourself to the Greatness That Lies Within*
- *Marketing in Your Underwear: Stripping Down to the Basics of Sales and Persuasion*
- *Peak Productivity: Design a Seven-Figure Business and a Lifestyle You Love by Following Through with Everything ... **and too many more to mention***

Success by Design: How Smart Entrepreneurs and Creators Build Lasting Habits

Connie Ragen Green

Connect with Connie Ragen Green further at Linktr.ee/ConnieRagenGreen

Success by Design: How Smart Entrepreneurs and Creators Build Lasting Habits

Dedication

"Success isn't built in grand moments of inspiration, but in the quiet, consistent choices you make every day. Design your habits with intention, and your future will be designed with great success, by design." ~ Connie Ragen Green

Just over two years ago, as of the date of this writing in January of 2026, I made a commitment to myself and to my online community: I would dedicate my work with the people who come to me for help, advice, and mentorship to serve them in a way that would allow *at least* one thousand people to achieve the goal of earning six-figures a year as an online entrepreneur, marketer, content writer and publisher, and course/product creator.

As of this writing, thirty-three people who have mentored with me over the past few years have now achieved and maintained this goal, and are on track to increase their income without spending any more time online. While I am excited at their progress, it is nowhere near where I thought we'd be by now.

What's missing? I now know that it is much more than desire, level of intelligence, and previous experience with marketing, although these are all helpful along your journey.

It all comes down to consistency, discipline, and habits. These three ways of acting, living, and reaching all of your goals and dreams are the focus of this book. I have been able to change my life completely by embracing them and what I am sharing with you in great detail here within these pages.

This book is dedicated to you if you know deep down inside that the entrepreneurial dream is right for you, you've grown weary of being an employee at the whim of a company and the economy, and are ready to create the life and the lifestyle you want for yourself and your family.

Imagine me taking your hand, placing it over my heart, and looking you directly in your eyes. That's how I think about the beginning of my relationship with you. Even if this is the very first time you and I are connecting, know that I'm already believing in you, and in the possibilities that you will achieve.

Precepts

Precepts are defined as guiding principles intended as rules of action and require being consistent and persistent, and taking action every day.

Each of these precepts are the philosophical pillars of *Success by Design: How Smart Entrepreneurs and Creators Build Lasting Habits.*

Each one represents a fundamental truth about what it really takes to achieve long-term success as a marketer, writer, or entrepreneur. Below is an expanded, detailed version of each precept — with both depth and practical insight so that you can include them in the book's early chapters, your workbook companion, or even your live teachings and workshops.

My Precepts... the Core Beliefs and Big Ideas for this book are as follows...

Precept 1: "Success isn't about working harder—it's about designing habits that make success inevitable."

Most new entrepreneurs believe that success will come if they hustle hard enough. Work longer hours. Push through exhaustion. Stay up late. Wake up early. Repeat.

But "work harder" is not a strategy — it's a short-term survival tactic.
What actually creates long-term success is *design.*

When your habits are intentionally created to support your goals, your success becomes automatic — the *natural* result of how you move through your day.

Imagine two marketers starting at the same place:

- One wakes up each morning reacting: checking social media, putting out fires, and trying to find motivation to write content.
- The other has a morning success routine that includes planning, writing for 30 minutes, and reviewing metrics.

After one month, the gap is noticeable.
After six months, it's undeniable.
After a year, it's a completely different life.

Designed habits remove friction.
They eliminate indecision.
They prevent overwhelm.
They ensure progress happens even on low-energy days.

This precept teaches you:
Success is not an event. It is the *cumulative effect* of the habits you architect.

Precept 2: "Discipline isn't a burden; it's a system for freedom and creativity."

Most people misunderstand discipline.
They think it means restriction, rigidity, or forcing yourself to do things you don't enjoy. But real discipline is the opposite — it creates *freedom.* Discipline…

- frees your mind from chaos
- frees your time from distractions
- frees your energy for what matters most
- frees your creativity to flourish

Writers feel the difference instantly.
Marketers feel it in their output.
Entrepreneurs feel it in their income and clarity.

Lack of discipline creates stress.
Last-minute deadlines, scattered focus, unfinished projects, financial worry.
Those are the real burdens.

Discipline *prevents* all of that. When you have a discipline system:

- You don't need to think about when to work.
- You don't debate whether to write today.
- You don't scramble to market your product.
- You don't waste time on low-value tasks.
  Everything flows, because your structure holds you.

Discipline is not the enemy of creativity.
It is the *incubator.*
Creativity thrives when your brain isn't drowning in disorganization.

Precept 3: "You don't need more motivation—you need a process and systems that keep you consistent."
If entrepreneurs waited for motivation:

- Chapters wouldn't get written
- Email campaigns wouldn't be created
- Products wouldn't be launched
- Content wouldn't be published
- Income wouldn't grow

Motivation is a spark — unreliable, unpredictable, fleeting; consistency is the engine.

Instead of waiting to "feel like it," smart creators build a process that ensures progress even on low-energy days.

A process is:

- a writing routine
- a marketing checklist
- a content calendar
- a daily top-three priorities list
- a Sunday planning ritual
- an automated workflow

When motivation fades — and it *always* will — process steps in and says:

"You don't need to feel inspired. You just need to follow the system."

This precept transforms readers because it releases them from the guilt of not feeling motivated.
It replaces emotion-based productivity with strategy-based productivity.

When you have a process, consistency is no longer a personality trait — it's a predictable result.

Precept 4: "Small, intentional habits create massive, lasting results."

The myth of entrepreneurship is that success comes from big breakthroughs. One launch. One viral post. One idea.

But real success comes from the *micro-actions* repeated relentlessly.

Examples:

Success by Design: How Smart Entrepreneurs and Creators Build Lasting Habits

- 20 minutes of writing every morning → a full book in a year
- Posting one piece of content daily → exponential visibility
- Reaching out to one potential client a day → consistent revenue
- Reading 10 pages each night → deepened expertise
- Planning your day each morning → increased clarity and output

Small habits stack.
They compound.
They multiply.

Most people quit because they underestimate the power of tiny steps.
They want results *now*, and when they don't see instant success, they assume they're failing.

But small actions, repeated, eventually cross a threshold where growth becomes exponential.
It's not immediate.
It's not glamorous.
But it is *transformational.*

This precept teaches readers:
Don't chase intensity. Chase consistency.

The small things you commit to today become the enormous achievements your future self stands on.

Precept 5: "What you do daily determines what you achieve permanently."

Your daily actions are your destiny.

Not your goals.
Not your dreams.
Not your intentions.
Not your emotional state.
Not your potential.

Your *habits.*

Your habits express your real priorities — not the ones you claim to have, but the ones you live.

If you write daily, you become an author.
If you market daily, you build an audience.
If you learn daily, you grow your expertise.
If you create daily, you build a business.
If you take small intentional steps daily, your progress becomes unstoppable.

What you do occasionally creates moments.
What you do daily creates your identity, your outcomes, and your future.

This precept reframes success as a *lifestyle,* not a moment. It's not about making massive, heroic efforts once in a while. It's about showing up consistently in small, meaningful ways that align with who you want to become.

Daily habits are the foundation of permanent success.

And here are five more Precepts that we will explore together, throughout this book and beyond...

Precept 6: Motivation Is Fleeting; Discipline Is Foundational and everlasting

Motivation is like a spark — powerful but temporary. It can ignite your enthusiasm, but it won't sustain your fire. Most new entrepreneurs and creators rely too heavily on motivation, waiting for the "right moment" or the "right mood" to take action. But motivation fades. It's tied to emotion, and emotions shift constantly.

Discipline, on the other hand, is steady. It's the engine that keeps moving forward even when the road gets steep. Discipline means honoring your commitments long after the excitement has worn off. It's not about feeling ready — it's about acting regardless of how you feel.

For entrepreneurs, discipline shows up in the mundane:

- *Writing every day, even when ideas don't flow easily.*
- *Posting your content even when engagement feels slow.*
- *Following up with potential clients, even when you'd rather avoid it.*

Every act of discipline strengthens your foundation. It builds resilience, reliability, and results. Motivation may get you started, but discipline ensures you arrive at your destination.

Key Lesson: Build your schedule around discipline, not emotion. Let structure carry you when inspiration won't.

Precept 7: Habits Create Freedom, Not Restrictions

Many people view habits as limiting — something that takes away spontaneity. In truth, habits are what give you *freedom*. When you automate your essential actions, you free your mental energy to focus on creativity, strategy, and innovation.

For entrepreneurs, habits reduce decision fatigue. Instead of asking, *"Should I work on my business today?"* your habits decide for you. The energy you save by not debating your next step can now be used to elevate your craft or deepen your client relationships.

Well-designed habits create stability and momentum. They anchor your day in intention and give you clarity about what truly matters. This structure is not a cage; it's a framework that supports your growth.

- When you have a habit of writing content every morning, your creativity expands.
- When you consistently review your business metrics, your confidence in decision-making grows.
- When you habitually learn, you evolve faster than the competition.

Key Lesson: Habits are the invisible architecture of freedom. They give you control over your time, your focus, and your results.

Precept 8: Small Actions, Repeated Consistently, Lead to Massive Results

Success is not built in giant leaps but in deliberate, consistent steps. Every extraordinary achievement you see — a bestselling book, a six-figure launch, a thriving personal brand — is the accumulation of small actions repeated over time.

It's the compound effect in motion.

- **One blog post becomes a library of resources.**
- **One email becomes a list of loyal subscribers.**
- **One video becomes a growing audience.**

Consistency magnifies impact. It transforms effort into momentum and momentum into mastery. The results you're chasing are simply the echo of actions you've taken consistently over time.

Many new entrepreneurs give up too soon because they underestimate the power of persistence. They plant seeds but

fail to water them long enough to see growth. The truth is that the rewards of consistency are *delayed but guaranteed* when the actions are aligned with your goals.

Key Lesson: Don't chase intensity; chase consistency. Your future success is being built in the small, unseen moments of today.

Precept 9: Identity Shapes Behavior—Act Like the Entrepreneur You Want to Become

True transformation begins not with what you *do* but with who you *believe yourself to be.* Your identity drives your behavior, and your behavior reinforces your identity — it's a continuous loop.

When you begin to see yourself as a professional, disciplined, successful entrepreneur, your daily choices begin to align with that vision. You naturally act in ways that reflect it — you make time for what matters, you hold yourself accountable, and you operate with confidence instead of hesitation.

This is why surface-level changes rarely last. If your habits conflict with your self-image, your subconscious will always pull you back to what feels "normal." To create lasting success, you must first *upgrade your identity.*

Ask yourself:

- **How would the entrepreneur I want to become structure their day?**
- **How would they respond to setbacks?**
- **What habits would they prioritize without fail?**

Each small choice to act "as if" reinforces your new identity until it becomes who you truly are.

Key Lesson: Lasting success comes from aligning your habits with your identity. Don't wait to become successful — start behaving like the person who already is.

Precept 10: Systems Beat Willpower—Structure Your Success

Willpower is a limited resource. It's unreliable under stress, fatigue, or distraction. Systems, however, are dependable — they remove the need for constant decision-making and self-control.

A system is simply a repeatable process that supports your goals. It's a way to make success *automatic* by designing your environment, routines, and tools to work in your favor.

For entrepreneurs and creators, effective systems might include:

- A weekly content creation plan with built-in deadlines.
- A structured marketing workflow that tracks leads and conversions.
- A morning routine that primes your focus and energy.

When you rely on systems instead of willpower, you reduce friction and increase follow-through. You stop fighting against yourself and start flowing with a framework that makes success predictable.

Key Lesson: Design your environment and systems to make good choices easy and consistent success inevitable.

Closing Reflection

Together, these 10 precepts form the heart of *Success by Design.* They remind entrepreneurs and creators that achievement isn't a mystery — it's a method.

Success by Design: How Smart Entrepreneurs and Creators Build Lasting Habits

You don't need more motivation, inspiration, or luck. You need a structure that supports your discipline, habits that reflect your identity, and systems that make consistency automatic.

That's what this book — and your new way of working — is all about.

Each one represents a fundamental truth about what it really takes to achieve long-term success as a marketer, writer, or entrepreneur. Below is an expanded, detailed version of each precept — with both depth and practical insight so that you can include them in the book's early chapters, your workbook companion, or even your live teachings and workshops.

Each of these encapsulates the core idea of intentional habit formation, discipline, and consistency as the key drivers of success for entrepreneurs, marketers, and writers. We will revisit these important precepts throughout this book, and each time you will move closer to embracing the changes you are making in your life experience.

Table of Contents

How Connie Ragen Green Created Her Own "Success by Design"

What You May Not Know That Will Help You to Move Forward with Your Own Great Success

"Be the change you wish to see in the world"
~ Mahatma Gandhi

Connie Ragen Green didn't begin her adult life imagining she'd become an author of more than thirty books, a mentor to thousands of entrepreneurs, or a woman who could build a business from a laptop and a stubborn belief that life could be different.

In fact, her early years looked nothing like the life she lives now. She grew up with more responsibilities than resources, and more dreams than opportunities. But she also grew up with grit — the kind of quiet determination that doesn't brag or boast, but simply whispers, *"You can do better... keep going."*

Before entrepreneurship entered the picture, Connie worked in a patchwork of jobs that kept the lights on but never lit her up. These included working as a claims adjuster for a national insurance carrier, and as a merchant teller at two banks, where she was robbed at gunpoint not once, but twice. She was a runaway at fifteen, married to a man ten years her senior at sixteen, and an instant step-mother. She worked as a waitress, a Hollywood bit-part extra, a substitute teacher, a real estate agent, and during numerous stretches of time, she held two full-time jobs simultaneously. She has stories — oh, she has stories! — most of them equal parts hilarious and heartbreaking, all of them proof that a single life can contain more chapters than anyone expects.

At age fifty, she decided to rewrite her story completely. She walked away from all her jobs — every last one — and started fresh as an online entrepreneur in a world she barely understood. She didn't know how to upload a file or send an email newsletter.

She didn't know what a domain name was or why people kept talking about "passive income" like it grew on trees. But she did know how to learn, how to show up, and how to keep taking small steps forward, even on days when the fear was louder than the progress. And it turns out, that was enough.

Connie built her first online business from scratch, one blog post, one article, one Call to Action (CTA), and one tiny win at a time. Within a few years, she replaced her old income. Then she surpassed it. Then she changed her life — not with some grand epiphany, but with the daily, deliberate habits she now teaches to others.

Today, Connie is known as a mentor who mixes wisdom with warmth, strategy with simplicity, and productivity with peace. Her work helps entrepreneurs — especially those starting later in life — discover that age is not a limit, uncertainty is not a flaw, and reinvention is always possible. She is proof that you can start fresh at forty, fifty, or seventy, and still build a business, a body of work, and a sense of confidence you once believed was out of reach.

And if you ever meet her in person, she'll greet you like an old friend, tell you a story that will make you laugh, and then gently remind you that your life is waiting — one habit, one moment, one brave step at a time.

Success by Design: How Smart Entrepreneurs and Creators Build Lasting Habits

"There are three solutions to every problem: accept it, change it, or leave it. If you can't accept it, change it. If you can't change it, leave it." ~ Unknown

This quote suggests three ways to handle a problem. If you cannot accept a situation, you should try to change it. If changing the situation is not possible, the final solution is to leave it behind. This framework encourages taking a proactive approach to challenges instead of feeling stuck or helpless, promoting either acceptance, action, or detachment as paths to resolution.

Accept it: Acknowledge the reality of the situation and finding peace with it, which can be the first step toward corrective action. It is about changing your perspective, not giving up.

Change it: If you cannot accept the current reality, the next step is to take action to alter the circumstances. This requires creativity and courage to change the situation or your perspective on it.

Leave it: If the problem cannot be changed and acceptance is not an option, walk away from the situation. This preserves your well-being and opens the door to new opportunities.

Foreword

Let me begin by saying that I am honored to be writing the Foreword for this book. Connie has become a force to be reckoned with and her heart is pure gold.

I've known Connie since our teenage years, and even back then, she had this unstoppable mix of curiosity, courage, and quiet determination. She was always the one asking deeper questions—the kind that made you stop and actually think about what mattered most in life. And while the rest of us were still figuring out what we wanted to do, Connie was already building habits that would later become the foundation of her success.

So, when she told me she was writing Success by Design: How Smart Entrepreneurs and Creators Build Lasting Habits, I smiled. It felt like the book she was always meant to write. Because Connie doesn't just teach success principles—she lives them. Every page in this book comes from real experience, trial and error, and the kind of wisdom that only comes from showing up day after day, even when it isn't easy.

What I love most about this book is how personal and practical it feels. Connie takes complex ideas—discipline, consistency, mindset—and makes them completely doable. It's like she's sitting across from you with a cup of coffee, walking you through the exact steps that will help you create habits that actually stick.

Reading this, you'll quickly see why so many people turn to her for guidance. She doesn't just help you work harder—she helps you work smarter, and with a sense of peace and purpose that most of us spend years chasing.

As her friend and as someone who's watched her evolve into a bestselling author, entrepreneur, and mentor, I can tell you this: you're in for something special. This isn't just a book

about building habits—it's a manual for building a life you love. Here's to designing your own success, one smart habit at a time.
~ Bill Arthur McCool

A Letter to the Reader

"Life is what happens to us while we're busy making other plans." ~ John Lennon

Dear Reader,

If you've opened this book, I want you to know something right away: this is not an accident. Something inside you is ready—ready to grow, ready to change, ready to become more consistent, more focused, and more aligned with the life you say you want to live.

This book was written for you if you've ever felt behind...
If you've ever wondered why you *know* what to do, yet struggle to do it consistently...
If you've ever started strong, only to lose momentum and quietly blame yourself.

I've been there.

I didn't write this book from a place of perfection. I wrote it from experience—earned experience. From years of starting over, rebuilding, and learning that success isn't created by dramatic breakthroughs, but by quiet, daily decisions most people never see.

Inside these pages, you won't find hype or empty motivation. What you *will* find is a clear, compassionate path forward—one that honors where you are now while guiding you toward where you want to be. This book is an invitation to stop forcing success and start *designing* it.

You don't need to become someone else to succeed.
You don't need more hours, more hustle, or more pressure.
You need habits that support you, discipline that frees you, and systems that carry you forward when motivation fades.

Success by Design: How Smart Entrepreneurs and Creators Build Lasting Habits

My hope is that as you read, you'll feel encouraged, challenged, and deeply understood. And more importantly, that you'll begin to trust yourself again—one small action at a time.

I'm honored you're here.

Let's begin.

With belief in you,

Connie

Preface – How This Book Came About

"The only way to make sense out of change is to plunge into it, move with it, and join the dance."
~ *Alan Wilson Watts*

Designing Success with Intention and Integrity

There comes a point in every entrepreneur's journey when hard work alone is no longer enough. We reach a crossroads where effort must give way to design—where our success depends not on how much we do, but on *how intentionally* we do it.

Success by Design was born from that realization.

In my early years as an entrepreneur, I was deeply committed but often overwhelmed. Like so many of us, I mistook activity for achievement. I would start strong—driven by excitement and inspiration—only to lose focus when motivation waned or distractions appeared. Over time, I began to recognize a pattern: my results were inconsistent because my habits were inconsistent.

That awareness was the turning point.

Once I began studying the science of habit formation, the psychology of discipline, and the art of deliberate practice, everything shifted. I discovered that the foundation of sustainable success isn't found in bursts of inspiration—it's built in the quiet consistency of daily action. Success, I realized, is not accidental. It's *architectural.*

This book represents the framework I've developed and refined over years of entrepreneurship, writing, and teaching others to take control of their results. It's a blueprint for designing a life and business that operate by intention, not impulse.

Throughout these chapters, you'll learn how to:

- Build habits that anchor your goals in daily action
- Develop the discipline to move forward even when the spark of motivation fades
- Replace perfectionism with steady progress
- Focus your attention in a world overflowing with noise and distraction
- Automate your success through simple, repeatable systems that support your values and vision

The purpose of *Success by Design* is not to add more to your already full plate—it's to help you create clarity, focus, and structure so you can work *smarter*, live *better*, and grow *steadily*.

It's a guide for entrepreneurs, creators, and professionals who are ready to rise above chaos and craft a more intentional path forward—one defined by purpose, productivity, and peace of mind.

Every principle and practice you'll find here has been tested in the real world—by me, by my clients, by those I mentor, and by countless individuals who wanted not just to succeed, but to *sustain* success. What I've learned is simple but profound: when your habits align with your highest priorities, success becomes not something you chase, but something you *embody*.

You have the ability to design the life and business you want—one deliberate choice, one refined habit, one consistent day at a time.

This book was born out of my own struggle to find structure, meaning, and momentum in a world that often felt chaotic. For years, I was doing all the "right" things—working hard, learning everything I could, setting goals—but somehow, lasting success and peace of mind always seemed just out of reach.

Then I discovered something powerful: success doesn't come from doing *more*—it comes from doing what *matters most*, consistently, and with intention. It comes from designing your days, your mindset, and your habits in a way that supports who you want to become.

Success by Design grew from my personal journey as an entrepreneur, author, and lifelong learner who decided to stop leaving success up to chance. I started asking deeper questions:

- What if the difference between feeling overwhelmed and feeling fulfilled wasn't effort—but design?
- What if we could make success *automatic* by creating systems that work for us instead of against us?
- And what if the habits we build today could quietly shape the life we've always wanted tomorrow?

This book is my answer to those questions.

I wrote *Success by Design* not just to share what I've learned, but to offer a roadmap for anyone who's tired of starting over, stopping short, or second-guessing their path. Whether you're an entrepreneur, a creative, or someone simply ready for change, my goal is to help you understand that success isn't a mystery—it's a method.

Inside, you'll find stories, science, and simple, actionable steps you can start using right away to:

- Build habits that actually stick
- Develop the discipline to stay the course when motivation fades
- Create consistency that compounds into meaningful results
- Eliminate distractions that drain your focus and energy
- Design a personalized system for success—one that reflects your values, dreams, and strengths

This isn't about becoming a different person. It's about uncovering the best version of who you already are—and aligning your daily actions with that truth.

If you've ever felt that spark inside you—the quiet knowing that you were meant for more—but weren't sure how to bridge the gap between where you are and where you want to be, this book is for you.

Success by Design: How Smart Entrepreneurs and Creators Build Lasting Habits

Success by Design isn't just a title—it's an invitation. To think bigger. To act smarter. To live with purpose. And most of all, to create the kind of success that feels right for *you.*

Thank you for trusting me to walk this path with you. My hope is that this book becomes your companion and guide—a blueprint for building a life you love, one habit at a time.

~ Connie Ragen Green

Introduction

"The price of success is hard work, dedication to the job at hand... whether we win or lose, we have applied the best of ourselves to the task at hand." ~ Vince Lombardi

This book isn't just about understanding habits—it's about implementing them. You'll learn how to start small, stay consistent, and achieve long-term success. My challenge to you as a reader: Take action and build your habit system today.

I will also be sharing valuable resources, tools, and next steps for designing a successful entrepreneurial life throughout these pages.

Success doesn't happen by accident—it happens by design. Entrepreneurs, marketers, and writers who consistently produce great work don't rely on fleeting motivation; they build systems, habits, and disciplines that make success inevitable.

"Success isn't about working harder—it's about designing habits that make success inevitable."

"Discipline isn't a burden; it's a system for freedom and creativity."

The book you are now reading, *Success by Design: How Smart Entrepreneurs and Creators Build Lasting Habits* is a practical guide to transforming your productivity, focus, and creativity through the power of intentional habits. Whether you're an online entrepreneur launching a business, a marketer looking to grow an audience, or a writer striving for consistency, this book will provide you with the tools to structure your daily routines, eliminate distractions, and stay committed to long-term success. An added benefit will be the confidence you gain along the way.

Success by Design: How Smart Entrepreneurs and Creators Build Lasting Habits

Success is defined differently by every person, yet the building blocks for success are pretty much universal. Then, how is it that success – financial, in terms of time freedom, and personal life satisfaction feels almost easy for some people while eluding others?

I believe this can be explained in terms of the habits, actions, beliefs, and personal interactions we have with others on a regular basis.

I'm an extreme introvert, meaning that I can enjoy my own company for extended periods of time. But the downside of this is that I miss out on forming lasting connections and friendships if I insist of keeping to myself.

What did I do to become a little more sociable in my day-to-day life? I reframed every action that took me closer to other human beings. I began to feel like a scientist exploring a newly appearing island in the Pacific Ocean. As the tip of the highest point appeared, I jumped into the water and introduced myself. The creative part of my mind had a mermaid appear, and she guided me on a tour of what was there for me to explore. Come along with me, if you will and let's explore this magical world together, shall we?

Prologue: Success on Your Terms, Regardless of Your Circumstances

I feel very lucky, blessed, and honored that you are reading this book. I am someone who believes in miracles and know for sure that we can all achieve all of the goals and dreams we have for our life experience. How am I so sure of these statements I'm making here? Because I was at the bottom of my game far more that anywhere near the top for the first fifty years of my life.

Because for much of my life, I was surviving, not thriving. I spent decades feeling as though I was running uphill with no clear destination in sight—working hard, doing what I thought I was *supposed* to do, yet always feeling a step behind where I wanted to be. I didn't lack effort. I lacked direction, systems, and the belief that success could be designed instead of chased.

There were long stretches when I felt invisible—to opportunity, to stability, and sometimes even to myself. I made choices based on necessity rather than intention. I worked multiple jobs, lived with uncertainty, and often wondered why success seemed to come so easily to others while I struggled just to stay afloat. Looking back now, I can see that I wasn't failing—I was learning. But at the time, it didn't feel that way.

What changed everything was not a single breakthrough moment, a lucky break, or a sudden stroke of confidence. It was a quiet realization that reshaped my entire life: I could choose differently. I could stop reacting to circumstances and start responding with intention. I could build habits that supported me instead of exhausting me. I could design a life aligned with who I wanted to become, not who I had been.

The miracles I believe in aren't sudden or supernatural. They are built slowly, through consistent action, disciplined choices, and a willingness to keep going when nothing seems to be working yet. They arrive when we show up for ourselves day after day, even when the results are invisible. Especially then.

If you are reading this book and wondering whether real change is still possible for you—whether you've waited too long, tried too many times, or failed too often—I want you to know this: I understand that feeling deeply. I lived it. And I am here to tell you that your past does not disqualify you from your future.

This book is not about overnight success or effortless transformation. It is about reclaiming your power, one habit at a time. It is about discipline that serves you, consistency that strengthens you, and systems that quietly carry you forward when motivation fades.

I wrote this book for the person I once was—the one who hoped but didn't yet know how to build. And I wrote it for the person you are today, standing at the edge of possibility, ready to design a life that finally feels like your own.

If my life can be transformed after fifty years of struggle, then yours can change too. And that is not a promise rooted in luck or circumstance—it is a promise rooted in truth, in practice, and in the extraordinary power of well-designed habits.

Section One: Defining Success on Your Terms

"Logic will get you from A to B. Imagination will take you everywhere." ~ Albert Einstein

Connie Ragen Green

When you think about success and being successful, what comes to mind? Do you imagine having unlimited income, time freedom, and traveling the world to visit your many friends and multiple homes in your favorite places? Or, is success more down to earth for you?

My long-time friend and mentor, Dr. Joe Vitale says that most people think if they have more time, more money, a better job, and more possessions, they'll be happy. That's the grand illusion! What you really want is right here in this moment. He shares everything you need to know in his book, _The Abundance Paradigm: Moving From the Law of Attraction to the Law of Creation_ and I highly recommend you read – or listen – to it to benefit as I have. It's also included in my Reading List at the end.

A Reflection for Conscious Entrepreneurs

What does _success really_ mean to you?

It's an important question—one that most people never pause long enough to ask themselves. It's easy to get swept up in society's version of success: big numbers, bigger launches, hustle, grind, recognition. But real fulfillment often comes when we stop chasing someone else's dream and start honoring our own.

True success is personal. For you, it might mean financial freedom. Or creative freedom. Or simply being able to work from anywhere, on your own time, doing work you believe in. Success might mean peace, presence, flexibility, or impact—not just profits.

When you define success on your own terms, everything changes. Your goals get clearer. Your priorities sharpen. You stop running toward someone else's finish line and start walking your own path—with intention and purpose.

So, let's slow down and ask...

What does "success" look like to me—if no one else were watching or judging?

(Paint a picture of your ideal day, week, or business. What are you doing? How do you feel?) For me, a house in the suburbs with a white picket fence did not resonate with what I wanted in my life experience and who I wanted to be. So, I kept dreaming until I found my ideal life, the life I wanted to create and live.

What parts of my current definition of success might be influenced by comparison to others and/or outside pressure? *(Is there anything I'm chasing just because I "should" or because someone else is?)*

What feelings do I associate with success?
(Joy? Freedom? Pride? Ease? Security? Fulfillment? List them.)

If I fully trusted myself, how would I define success right now in this season of my life or business?

What is one small shift I can make today to align more with *my* definition of success?

Success doesn't have to be loud and all consuming; It just has to be *yours*. Take your time. Reflect. Redefine. Then rebuild your life and business from that truth. Let's continue with your journey to great success, by design, on your terms, and in your time. Stick with me here as we go more deeply and intentionally into what I'm sharing with you in this book.

Before You Begin

Before you turn the page and dive into Chapter One, I invite you to pause—just for a moment.

This book is not meant to be rushed through, skimmed, or consumed passively. It's designed to be *experienced*. The ideas within it will work only if you're willing to engage with them honestly and apply them gently but consistently.

Here's what I want you to know before you begin:

First, **you do not need to be perfect** to benefit from this book. You don't need ideal circumstances, endless time, or unwavering motivation. You only need a willingness to start where you are—and to take small, intentional steps forward.

Second, **this book is about responsibility, not self-blame**. Taking responsibility for your habits is an act of empowerment. It means you recognize that while you may not control everything that has happened to you, you *do* have influence over what happens next.

Third, **progress will come from consistency, not intensity**. You may feel inspired at times—and challenged at others. Both are part of the process. When things feel uncomfortable, it often means something important is shifting.

As you read, I encourage you to reflect, write notes, and revisit sections that resonate. Let the ideas settle. Let them challenge old assumptions. Let them shape new routines and, over time, a new identity.

Most of all, give yourself permission to believe this truth:

Your future is not built in one bold moment—but in the habits you practice every day.

When you're ready, turn the page.

Literally, your next chapter begins now.

Chapter One

The Success Formula: Why Habits, Discipline, and Consistency Matter

"Habit, if not resisted, soon becomes necessity."
~ Saint Augustine

This opening chapter sets the foundation for the entire book. It is intended to introduce you to the importance of intentional habit formation, the role of discipline, and why consistency—not fleeting motivation—is the key to lasting success.

The goal of this first chapter is to help you achieve your first mindset shift, helping you to see that success is not about luck or talent but about what you do consistently every single day.

Success doesn't happen by accident—it happens by design. Entrepreneurs, marketers, and writers who consistently produce great work don't rely on fleeting motivation; they build systems, habits, and disciplines that make success inevitable.

What I'm sharing with you in this book, *Success by Design: How Smart Entrepreneurs and Creators Build Lasting Habits* is a practical strategy to transforming your productivity, focus, and creativity through the power of intentional habits. Whether you're an online entrepreneur launching a business, a marketer looking to grow an audience, or a writer striving for consistency, this book will provide you with the tools to structure your daily routines, eliminate distractions, and stay committed to long-term success.

My advice to you, based on my own experience and that of my readers is to take your time with this book. Instead of jumping around, go through it one chapter at a time. Take some notes, pause to reflect, and talk to another human about what is coming up for you. We all tend to push down our feelings into a dark place where we hope they will never surface. Instead, keep these emotions close to the surface and allow them to bubble up to the place in you where noting can be forgotten, set aside, or overlooked. I'm been where I'm sending you many times, and each time the pain and fear and shame have worked themselves into joy and love and opportunities and results, all leading to a level of success I did not know even existed when I started out.

The Not So Secret, Secret Formula

A formula for success... What a wonderful idea! Could there truly exist a formula for us to be able to achieve all of our goals and dreams, both for our businesses and our personal lives more easily? Yes, but with the caveat that you will need to engage in a series of mindset shifts to make this happen for you as quickly and joyously as possible.

As I mentioned at the beginning of this chapter, the goal here is to help you achieve your first mindset shift, helping you to see that success is not about luck or talent but about what you do consistently every single day. If I had known this earlier in my life, oh, the places I could have gone!

In truth, I believe that we are always exactly at the right place and that we must endure the journey to develop the mindset that will eventually take us to paradise on Earth. Our struggles give us strength and character, and a greater appreciation for what we can achieve.

This book is your blueprint. Use it not just to reach your goals, but to elevate the way you think, act, and live. Think about where you've been, where you want to go, and the lifestyle that has your name written all over it. Make some notes and take a few minutes to reflect before you continue reading...

LIFESTYLE is the acronym I have chosen for this book. It is my hope that you will embrace at least some of what I am sharing with you here, and in a way that will shift your thinking and lead you to the life and lifestyle you want and deserve...

Success isn't an accident—it's a result of consistent action, aligned priorities, and powerful habits. If you're an entrepreneur or content creator, you already know the importance of strategy and hustle. But what really makes the difference over time?

Your *LIFESTYLE*—the habits you live by each day.

Here's how to break it down and build a lifestyle that supports your goals, one powerful letter at a time:

L – Learn Daily

Commit to lifelong learning. Whether it's reading, listening to podcasts, or taking online courses, continual growth keeps your edge sharp and your mind open.

The most successful entrepreneurs never stop learning. Whether it's reading books, listening to podcasts, taking online courses, or even just reflecting on your own experiences— every day presents a new opportunity to grow.

***Pro Tip:* Block out at least 20–30 minutes per day for intentional learning. It could be early in the morning, on your commute, or during a lunch break. Don't just consume—take notes and capture insights that are actionable.**

I – Implement Quickly - Ideas are great, but execution wins. Successful entrepreneurs don't just consume knowledge—they apply it swiftly and refine it as they go. Too many people fall into the trap of "learning paralysis"— endlessly consuming information without putting it to use. The most effective habit builders are action takers. Don't wait until it's perfect. Test, tweak, and move forward.

Challenge Yourself:* After every learning session, ask: *What's one thing I can try today based on what I just learned?

Success by Design: How Smart Entrepreneurs and Creators Build Lasting Habits

F – Focus Relentlessly

Distractions are the enemy of progress. Cultivate deep focus on your highest-priority goals and protect your time fiercely.

Focus is your superpower in an age of distraction. As an entrepreneur, your to-do list never ends, so you have to learn how to focus on what *really* moves the needle.

Try This: Use time-blocking to schedule deep work. Turn off notifications, close extra tabs, and set a timer. Even 60 minutes of focused effort can produce more results than 3 hours of scattered multitasking.

E – Eliminate Excuses

Drop the stories holding you back. Take radical ownership of your time, choices, and outcomes.

Excuses keep you stuck. Whether it's "I don't have time," "I'm not ready," or "I'm not good at marketing"—these are stories we tell ourselves to stay in the comfort zone. Excuses may feel valid, but they rarely move you forward.

Mindset Shift: Reframe excuses as opportunities. Instead of "I don't have time," try "This isn't a priority—do I want it to be?"

S – Simplify Systems

Complexity kills momentum. Build systems and routines that are repeatable, automated when possible, and easy to maintain.

Complexity is the enemy of consistency. When your systems are too complicated, you'll struggle to maintain them. The best habits are simple, sustainable, and scalable.

Quick Tip: Pick one system in your business (e.g., email marketing, content creation, invoicing) and ask: *How can I make this easier or more automatic?*

T – Track Your Progress

What gets measured, gets improved. Use metrics to see what's working and adjust accordingly. Even small wins compound.

If you're not measuring it, you're not improving it. Tracking helps you stay accountable and motivated, especially when progress feels slow. Whether it's tracking revenue, habits, or milestones—numbers tell a story.

Tool It Up: Use a simple habit tracker, spreadsheet, or even a whiteboard to visualize your progress. Celebrate small wins—they add up fast.

Y – State Your 'Why' First

Start with purpose. Remind yourself daily why you're building your business—it fuels discipline when motivation fades.

Your "why" is the fuel behind every habit and hustle. It keeps you going when motivation runs dry. Knowing why you're doing something creates emotional connection and long-term drive.

Get Clear: Write down your "why" and keep it visible—on your desk, your phone background, or your journal. Revisit it often, especially on hard days.

L – Lead Yourself

Before you can lead a team or a movement, you must lead yourself with integrity, discipline, and clarity of vision.

Entrepreneurship requires leadership. And leadership starts with how you show up for yourself—your mindset, your habits, your decisions. Leading yourself well means staying in integrity with your goals, even when no one's watching.

Ask Yourself: Would I follow me today? If not, what needs to shift?

E – Energize Mind & Body

Success is a marathon. Prioritize sleep, movement, hydration, and mindfulness so your energy supports your ambition.

All the strategy in the world won't help if you're exhausted or burnt out. Your body and brain are your greatest assets— fuel them well. Sleep, hydration, movement, and mindfulness aren't luxuries; they're performance tools.

Wellness Habit: Start small. Go for a daily 10-minute walk, hydrate first thing in the morning, or add a 2-minute breathing break to your routine.

Success by Design: How Smart Entrepreneurs and Creators Build Lasting Habits

Success isn't just about how hard you work—it's about how smart you live. The LIFESTYLE you choose will either carry you forward or keep you stuck.

Start with just one letter today. Build one new habit. Then layer another. Before you know it, your daily lifestyle *is* the success you're chasing.

Want to go deeper? I'm working on a free guide to help you implement these LIFESTYLE habits into your daily routine—complete with checklists, habit trackers, and prompts. Want early access? Let me know!

The Myth of Talent vs. The Reality of Daily Habits

Many people believe that successful entrepreneurs, writers, and marketers have an innate talent that gives them an edge. However, research shows that success is not about talent—it's about consistent effort applied over time.

If you are looking for the key to being successful, many people ponder the contributions of natural talent vs daily habits in this regard.

And if truth be told, both talent and habits are major contributing factors to the success of a person. Talent is the natural ability to perform exceptionally in a particular field, whereas consistent habits are what keep personal and business growth alive and thriving.

Even if highly talented people have a head start, developing and maintaining daily habits is more important than talent. Why? Hardworking people would likely surpass naturally gifted individuals when it comes down to perseverance.

Let's review the Case studies of some successful entrepreneurs, authors, and creators who started with no experience but built their success through deliberate habits and daily discipline. The people I have chosen are from a wide range of backgrounds, beliefs, dreams, and goals. While I hope you will resonate with at least a couple of them, you may find that there are already people whose story continues to be meaningful to you.

Sir Richard Branson

British businessman Richard Branson may be synonymous with entrepreneurial success, but he came from a humble beginning, at one point believing he was "the dumbest person at school."

His first attempt at business was by founding Student Magazine which he launched in 1966. The youth magazines of that period were too "boring" and his ideas for the magazine were too "revolutionary" for that time. So, he created a space that will allow fresh and new content that will interest the student audience.

At first, he was very short of cash, but after a stroke of luck, which saw him inherit £100 (which is the equivalent of $1500 today), he was able to pay his bills and keep the publication going for a few issues. The magazine was a success, and from this tiny acorn, the seeds were sown for his future success. He's now the founder of brands including Virgin Records, Virgin Atlantic, Virgin Money and his latest venture, Virgin Galactic — which he believes will be the world's first space tourism company.

His advice to future billionaires in the making is simple: don't wait to start until you have all your investments in place. He says he often receives letters from start-ups saying: "I need x amount of money to get started." But he believes this is not the way to start.

"There's no doubt it can be easier to achieve lofty ambitions if you already have financial backing," he said, "but in many cases you don't need lots of money to start a business. Rather than commit to pricey premises you can set up online with no technical expertise using a website builder, and start selling from your kitchen table."

Success by Design: How Smart Entrepreneurs and Creators
Build Lasting Habits

Branson must know what he's talking about. His personality and unconventional business style has won him awards, global fame and fortune; he is now said to be worth $4.2 billion.

Joyce Hall

I first heard about Joyce Hall and Hallmark cards from my mother when I was a child. Mom had worked for this company in St. Joseph, Missouri when she first graduated from high school in 1935.

At just 18 years old, Joyce C. Hall started a greeting card company that would go on to become a multi-million-dollar empire. With hard work and determination, Hallmark became one of the most successful businesses in the world. Today, we will be taking a closer look at his story and what made him so successful.

Early Years and Major Setback

He stepped off a train in Kansas City in 1910 with only two shoeboxes of greeting cards and a dream. Soon after he took on his brother as a partner to help him run the business and had a major setback in 1915 when the entire stock of cards was destroyed in a fire. They took the only item they had left, the Safe, and opened shop again, and now they were in $17,000's of debt. But Joyce was never willing to give up and had the determination to succeed with his dream.

Undeterred by the loss, Hallmark rebounded and began to grow at an incredible rate after figuring out what the customer was looking for. People didn't just want a postcard that anyone could see what they wrote. They wanted privacy, so the Hall brothers started creating high-quality cards with an envelope. And the fire had ended up being a blessing soon after.

The hall brothers decided to go in a different direction after the fire and invested in printing presses so they could create their own greeting cards in late 1915.

During the peak Christmas season of 1917, the hall brothers had started in the second product line of the modern gift wrap. They couldn't keep it in stock, so they decided to add gift wrap to the printing press.

1928 was the deciding year of what we know as the Hallmark symbol.

That little symbol on all the Hallmark cards and now on so many different things like movies. This is very interesting to me, as I had never heard this story before, even from my mother. I just figured it was due to the last name "Hall" which was why they chose this.

Hallmark defined — "a distinctive feature, especially one of excellence." Of high quality.

J.C. Hall had seen that goldsmiths used this on gold for a mark of high quality. He liked that it also had his last name in it and that is when he became an innovator in marketing the brand that's stood for over 100 years.

By the time he was in his early twenties, Joyce Hall had built a successful business. He continued to grow the company, and by the end of the 1920s, Hallmark was one of the largest greeting card companies in the United States. In 1930, he took the company public and became a millionaire.

Joyce Hall's success was due to his hard work and dedication. He was always looking for new ways to grow his business and make his products better. He was also a master of marketing, and he knew how to reach his customers. His story is an inspiration to all entrepreneurs.

By the time Joyce C. Hall retired in 1979, his greeting card company had become a multi-million-dollar empire with more than 100 stores across America. What started as a small business venture turned into one of the most successful companies in the world. Hall's story is a reminder that anything is possible with hard work and determination. Perhaps it was the stories that my mother told me about him during my formative years gave me some mental resilience as I got older.

Success by Design: How Smart Entrepreneurs and Creators Build Lasting Habits

Oprah Winfrey

Oprah Winfrey is a famous American media executive, actress, talk show host, philanthropist, and businesswoman. She is best known for her talk show, the Oprah Winfrey Show, which she hosted from 1986 to 2011. Oprah is one of the most successful people in the world and has been ranked as the richest African American of the 20th century. She has also been listed as one of the most influential people in the world by Time magazine.

Oprah is an inspiration to many, and her journey from struggles to success is an inspiration to many. She exemplifies how hard work and determination can take you to great heights.

Early Life Struggles

Oprah was born in 1954 in Mississippi to a single teenage mother. She had a difficult childhood, facing poverty and abuse. At nine, she was sent to live with her father, who provided a strict and disciplined upbringing. Despite her struggles, Oprah was a bright student and was accepted into a prestigious school.

At the age of 14, Oprah was raped and abused by family members and other people in her community. Despite these traumatic experiences, Oprah managed to persevere and keep her focus on her studies. She was awarded a full scholarship to Tennessee State University, where she studied communication.

After graduating from college, Oprah started her career as a news anchor in Baltimore. She quickly rose to fame for her passionate and informed reporting. In 1984, she was offered her television show, The Oprah Winfrey Show, which would become one of the most successful talk shows in history.

The Oprah Winfrey Show ran for 25 years and was the highest-rated talk show in the United States. During her show, Oprah interviewed some of the biggest celebrities, politicians, and public figures in the world. She also covered important topics such as racism, poverty, and violence.

In the late 1990s, Oprah launched her production company, Harpo Productions. Through Harpo, Oprah produced her television shows, films, and books. She also launched her own magazine, O, The Oprah Magazine, one of the world's most successful magazines.

In addition to her television shows, Oprah started her radio show, Oprah Radio, and launched her television network, OWN: The Oprah Winfrey Network. Through these outlets, Oprah has reached millions of people around the world and has become one of the most influential media moguls in the world.

Oprah's Philanthropy

Oprah has used her success to help others. She has established the Oprah Winfrey Foundation, which helps fund charitable causes worldwide. Oprah has donated millions of dollars to educational, environmental, health, and social causes through her foundation.

She has also established the Oprah Winfrey Leadership Academy for Girls in South Africa, providing young women with education and resources. The academy has been credited with helping the lives of thousands of young women in South Africa.

Winfrey has used her success to launch successful business ventures. In 2009, she launched her clothing line, O, The Oprah Magazine Collection. The collection was a huge success and sold in stores worldwide.

Oprah also launched her skincare line called O, The Oprah Magazine Skincare. The line was a huge success and was praised for using natural ingredients. In addition, Oprah has launched her own books and several online and in-person programs that have helped countless people from around the world to improve their lives. She has also become a venture capitalist, investing in several successful startups.

Success by Design: How Smart Entrepreneurs and Creators Build Lasting Habits

Eliza Lucas Pinckney

In the late colonial era, fathers supported their daughters by helping them find husbands and funding dowries—and perhaps by giving them an education that would help them oversee a large household. Eliza Pinckney's father instead handed his 16-year-old daughter the job of managing his struggling rice plantations in South Carolina, while he returned to the West Indies. Her dowry included the ability to draw on her father's business connections; a collection of seeds he sent her from Antigua and a group of enslaved people whose intensive labor facilitated her business's success.

Those assets turned out to be an auspicious combination for a young woman like Pinckney, whose favorite subject at her British finishing school had been botany rather than French or needlework. Pinckney experimented with alfalfa, ginger, hemp and flax, but struck gold when she found a way to develop a new strain of indigo that English textile mills—in constant search of new dyes—eagerly snapped up. Within a handful of years, indigo became the colony's second-largest cash crop and Pinckney became wealthy enough to reject suitors recommended by her father, instead selecting her own husband. George Washington served as a pallbearer at her funeral in 1793.

Andrew Carnegie

Andrew Carnegie, whose life became a rags-to-riches story, was born into modest circumstances on November 25, 1835, in Dunfermline, Scotland, the second of two sons of Will, a handloom weaver, and Margaret, who did sewing work for local shoemakers. In 1848, the Carnegie family (who pronounced their name "carNEgie") moved to America in search of better economic opportunities and settled in Allegheny City (now part of Pittsburgh), Pennsylvania. Andrew Carnegie, whose formal education ended when he left Scotland, where he had no more than a few years' schooling, soon found employment as a bobbin boy at a cotton factory, earning $1.20 a week.

Ambitious and hard-working, he went on to hold a series of jobs, including messenger in a telegraph office and secretary and telegraph operator for the superintendent of the Pittsburgh division of the Pennsylvania Railroad. In 1859, Carnegie succeeded his boss as railroad division superintendent. While in this position, he made profitable investments in a variety of businesses, including coal, iron and oil companies and a manufacturer of railroad sleeping cars.

After leaving his post with the railroad in 1865, Carnegie continued his ascent in the business world. With the U.S. railroad industry then entering a period of rapid growth, he expanded his railroad-related investments and founded such ventures as an iron bridge building company (Keystone Bridge Company) and a telegraph firm, often using his connections to win insider contracts. By the time he was in his early 30s, Carnegie had become a very wealthy man.

In the early 1870s, Carnegie co-founded his first steel company, near Pittsburgh. Over the next few decades, he created a steel empire, maximizing profits and minimizing inefficiencies through ownership of factories, raw materials and transportation infrastructure involved in steel making. In 1892, his primary holdings were consolidated to form Carnegie Steel Company.

After Carnegie sold his steel company, the diminutive titan, who stood 5'3", retired from business and devoted himself full-time to philanthropy. In 1889, he had penned an essay, "The Gospel of Wealth," in which he stated that the rich have "a moral obligation to distribute [their money] in ways that promote the welfare and happiness of the common man." Carnegie also said, "The man who dies thus rich dies disgraced."

Carnegie eventually gave away some $350 million (the equivalent of billions in today's dollars), which represented the bulk of his wealth. Among his philanthropic activities, he funded the establishment of more than 2,500 public libraries around the globe, donated more than 7,600 organs to churches worldwide and endowed organizations (many still in existence today) dedicated to research in science, education, world peace and other causes.

Among his gifts was the $1.1 million required for the land and construction costs of Carnegie Hall, the legendary New York City concert venue that opened in 1891. The Carnegie Institution for Science, Carnegie Mellon University and the Carnegie Foundation were all founded thanks to his financial gifts. A lover of books, he was the largest individual investor in public libraries in American history.

Madam C.J. Walker

The daughter of formerly enslaved workers-turned-sharecroppers, Sarah Breedlove triumphed over not only sexism but racism in her journey to become the country's first Black self-made woman millionaire. After selling door to door for Annie Turnbo Malone, another pioneer of Black hair products, she developed and marketed her own line of hair products and straighteners under the brand name "Madam Walker's Wonderful Hair Grower." (Walker was a married name and "Madam" sounded French, she said, and more respectful to Black women.)

After growing up in deep poverty and spending her early years picking cotton and working as a laundress, Walker built a business that not only earned her great personal wealth, but financially empowered more than 40,000 Black women as sales agents. In her final year of life, her earnings topped $500,000 ($8.7 million in today's dollars) and her widespread property holdings included a country estate in Irvington, New York designed by pioneering Black architect Vertner Tandy. She became known for her philanthropic and political endeavors, using her money to promote Black rights and equality.

Gabrielle "CoCo" Chanel: A Rebel Entrepreneur Before the Word Existed

From Orphanage to Icon: The Power of Origin Stories

Gabrielle Bonheur Chanel was born in 1883 into poverty. After her mother died, her father abandoned her and placed her in an orphanage run by nuns. This detail matters deeply for entrepreneurs:

- She learned sewing there—what later became her core skill
- She absorbed discipline, simplicity, and structure
- The stark black-and-white aesthetic of the convent later showed up in her brand

Entrepreneur lesson:
Your beginnings do not disqualify you—they often *design* you. Skills learned in survival mode can become signature strengths later.

Reinvention Is a Business Strategy

She reinvented herself repeatedly. The nickname **"CoCo"** came from her brief attempt at being a café singer—*not* a roaring success, but a stepping stone.

Instead of clinging to a failing dream, she pivoted.

Entrepreneur lesson:
You are allowed to change direction without losing credibility. Reinvention is not quitting—it's refining.

She Solved a Real Problem (Before "Pain Points" Were a Thing)

At a time when women were suffocating in corsets and elaborate clothing, Chanel introduced:

- Simple jersey fabrics (previously used for men's underwear)

- Comfortable silhouettes
- Practical elegance over decoration

She didn't chase trends—**she removed friction from women's lives**.

Entrepreneur lesson:

The best businesses don't add more. They *simplify*. Look for what feels heavy, outdated, or uncomfortable—and redesign it.

Chanel Didn't Just Sell Products—She Sold a Philosophy

Her famous quote says it all:

"Luxury must be comfortable, otherwise it is not luxury."

She wasn't just selling clothes or perfume—she was selling:

- Freedom
- Modern womanhood
- Confidence
- Independence

Entrepreneur lesson:

People don't buy what you sell. They buy the *belief* behind it. Your philosophy is part of your product.

Chanel No. 5: Scalable Thinking Before Digital Products

Chanel No. 5 wasn't just a fragrance—it was **scalable income**.

- She partnered strategically (even controversially) to expand distribution
- She created a product that could reach millions without her physical presence
- It outlived trends, seasons, and even her own lifetime

Entrepreneur lesson:
True wealth comes from assets that work while you're not present. Think beyond time-for-money.

Ruthless Focus on Brand Identity
Chanel controlled her image fiercely:
- The interlocking C's
- The little black dress
- Pearls
- Timeless, minimalist elegance

She understood **brand consistency before marketing textbooks existed**.

Entrepreneur lesson:
Clarity beats complexity. When people can describe your brand in one sentence, you've won.

She Broke Rules—and Lived with the Consequences
Chanel wore trousers, rejected corsets, and borrowed from men's fashion. She also lived a controversial life and made choices that still spark debate.

She was:
- Admired
- Criticized
- Imitated
- Misunderstood

Entrepreneur lesson:
Visibility attracts both admiration and judgment. Playing safe rarely builds a legacy.

Longevity Through Timelessness
Chanel famously said:
"Fashion fades, only style remains the same."
She designed for *endurance*, not virality.

Success by Design: How Smart Entrepreneurs and Creators Build Lasting Habits

Entrepreneur lesson:
Build your business on principles, not trends. What you create should still matter years from now.

I will encourage you to research the people in our history that have defined success on their own terms over the centuries, and whom will continue to inspire and motivate generations to come. I believe that history is a valuable topic to explore and question, as a way to not repeat mistakes of the past.

The "Iceberg Illusion" is not understanding that the end result of success is based upon the years of habits that built it.

Understanding the Iceberg Illusion

The "Iceberg Illusion" is a metaphor that illustrates how the visible part of success — the achievements, recognition, and results that others see — represents only a small fraction of the whole story. Like the tip of an iceberg rising above the surface, what's visible to the world is supported by an enormous, unseen foundation beneath the waterline.

In the context of habits, discipline, and consistency, this illusion reminds us that:

What people see as "overnight success" is actually the visible outcome of years of invisible effort.

Breaking Down the Illusion: The Tip of the Iceberg — What Others See

Public achievements: the book published, the business launched, the awards won, the audience built.

The appearance of confidence, talent, or luck.

Success that seems effortless — as if it "just happened."

This is what the world notices. It's the outcome, not the process. And without context, it can create false perceptions — leading others to believe that success is quick, easy, or innate.

Below the Surface – What Actually Built It
Beneath every visible success is a massive foundation of invisible habits and choices, including:

Early mornings and late nights spent refining skills.

Thousands of small, often uncelebrated actions taken with discipline.

Failures, course corrections, and lessons learned through persistence.

Sacrifices made in private to honor long-term goals.

The emotional resilience to keep going when no one is watching or applauding.

This is where habits live — in the unseen daily repetition that slowly shapes ability, confidence, and momentum.

The Core Truth of the Iceberg Illusion

Success isn't a single event. It's the cumulative result of consistent behaviors practiced over time.

People often underestimate this because they focus only on results. But every success story — in entrepreneurship, writing, or creative work — is actually a habit story.

That bestselling author? Years of writing daily when no one was reading.

That thriving online entrepreneur? Countless small marketing actions, content pieces, and relationship-building moments compounded over time.

That disciplined creator? A system of habits designed to make excellence inevitable.

Why It Matters for New Entrepreneurs and Creators

Understanding the Iceberg Illusion helps newer entrepreneurs:

Stay grounded — realizing that mastery and momentum come with time.

Stay patient — success grows in the dark before it shines in the light.

Stay consistent — small habits today are the foundation for visible results tomorrow.

Avoid comparison — because everyone's iceberg has a different size, shape, and timeline.

The Takeaway

If you're building your business, writing your book, or developing your craft — remember this truth:

The success you dream of will one day be the "tip of the iceberg."

But right now, you are building the part that truly matters — the unseen foundation of habits, discipline, and consistency that will hold everything up.

People tend to see the success of someone (the tip of the iceberg) but do not see all the stages of mistakes, persistence, failures, etc. (the lower half of the iceberg/under the water) that they go through to achieve the success which is the stages of a growth mindset.

Most 'overnight' successes actually took many years and a lot of hard work, persistence, sacrifice, and even multiple failures. But, because we only see the end result, it's easy to think that success is easy, or should arrive quickly. This is known as the 'Iceberg Illusion'.

The power of deliberate practice: How breaking down skills into daily, structured practice leads to mastery.

Success is not determined by chance; it's earned through choice. You can choose to embrace these habits and be a top achiever. It takes time and dedication; eventually, your numbers will catch up with your commitment.

Saint Augustine famously said, "Habit, if not resisted, soon becomes a necessity." Ask yourself, "Which habits are worth embracing?" Planning a call is a habit, as is NOT planning a call. Resist the wrong habits and embrace the right ones. Since habits become a necessity, ensure you choose the right ones.

It's not just talent or motivation; habits set top achievers apart from the crowd. Top achievers make it a habit to do what others deem a pain, boring, or simply a waste of time.

Why Motivation is Unreliable and Discipline is Essential

Many people believe that motivation is the key to success. They wait for inspiration to strike before they take action, believing that they need to "feel" ready before they start working on their goals. However, this approach is flawed because motivation is a fleeting emotion, while discipline is a system that ensures long-term success—even when you don't feel like showing up.

Motivation is a feeling, and feelings are inconsistent. Waiting until you "feel" like working will result in wasted time and missed opportunities.

Motivation is Temporary and Unpredictable

Motivation is based on emotions, which fluctuate daily. Some days, you wake up feeling energized and excited. Other days, you don't want to do anything.

Many people believe that motivation is the key to success. They wait for inspiration to strike before they take action, believing that they need to "feel" ready before they start working on their goals. However, this approach is flawed because motivation is a fleeting emotion, while discipline is a system that ensures long-term success—even when you don't feel like showing up.

If you rely on motivation, your productivity will be inconsistent because you'll only work when you feel like it.

External vs. Internal Motivation:

External motivation (money, praise, rewards) can give short-term energy but often fades over time.

Internal motivation (purpose, passion, vision) is more sustainable but still requires a system to keep you on track.

The "Waiting for Inspiration" Trap:

Writers often wait for the perfect mood to write, and entrepreneurs wait for the right idea to take action.

The truth: Taking action creates motivation. When you start working, motivation follows—not the other way around. I like to think of this as "inspired action" and act it almost immediately when it strikes me.

Discipline is a System and a Habit: It's *NOT* a Mood

I think of discipline as being a system and a habit, not a mood. Successful entrepreneurs and writers show up even when they don't feel like it. I love the quote for writers that says... "I only write when I am inspired, and I see to it that I'm inspired at nine o'clock every morning." ~ Unknown.

Successful people rely on discipline, not motivation, to stay productive.

- Athletes train even when they don't feel like it.
- Writers write even when they don't have the perfect idea.
- Entrepreneurs work on their business even when they feel uninspired.

Discipline removes decision fatigue. When you rely on motivation, every day becomes a mental negotiation: *"Do I feel like doing this today?"* When you develop discipline, the decision is already made. You don't ask yourself *if* you'll do the work—you just do it.

Example: The Professional vs. The Amateur Mindset

- Amateurs work when they feel inspired.
- Professionals work on a schedule, no matter what.
- A pro doesn't ask, *"Do I feel like doing this today?"* They just show up and do the work.

The "Show Up Rule" - Taking Action Creates Motivation

Success by Design: How Smart Entrepreneurs and Creators Build Lasting Habits

- Most people believe that motivation leads to action, but in reality: Action → Progress → Motivation
- When you take even a small action, you create momentum. Progress leads to motivation, which fuels more action.
- The "Show Up Rule" means committing to starting, even if you only do a small amount.

Example: Commit to 5 minutes. If you don't feel like writing, start with a single sentence. If you don't feel like exercising, commit to 5 minutes of movement. At least 99% of the time, once you start, you'll keep going.

How to Build Discipline and Make It Automatic

Since discipline is more reliable than motivation, the goal is to make discipline effortless. You do this by designing habits and systems that make success inevitable.

- **1.** Set a non-negotiable schedule.

Write at the same time every day.
Market your business at a consistent time.
Develop a structured work routine.

- **2.** Use environmental design.

Set up your workspace to remove distractions.
Make starting easy: Have your tools and materials ready in advance.
Reduce temptation (e.g., use website blockers if you're prone to procrastination).

- **3. Automate your habits.**

Stack new habits onto existing ones (habit stacking).

Use reminders, alarms, or habit trackers.
Make small, incremental improvements daily.

- **4. Have an accountability system.**

Work with a partner, coach, or community.
Track your progress and review it weekly.
Reward yourself for consistency, not just results.

Ironically, discipline gives you more freedom than motivation ever will. When you rely on motivation, you're a prisoner to your emotions—your work and success are at the mercy of how you feel that day. But when you have discipline, you are in control. You do the work, and success becomes inevitable.

You'll discover that discipline leads to freedom... time freedom, financial freedom, creative freedom.

Ironically, discipline gives you more freedom than motivation ever will. When you rely on motivation, you're a prisoner to your emotions—your work and success are at the mercy of how you feel that day. But when you have discipline, you are in control. You do the work, and success becomes inevitable. Implement the "Just Start" Principle, where taking action leads to motivation (not the other way around).

Be willing to take the time each day to build the habit of showing up daily, even on bad days.

How to reframe discipline as a muscle that gets stronger with consistent use...

The Power of Compounding Small Actions Over Time

One of the biggest reasons people struggle with consistency is because they underestimate the power of small actions. They think success requires big, dramatic efforts when in reality, small, consistent actions, repeated over time, lead to massive results. This is the power of compounding—a principle that applies not only to finance but also to habits, skills, and success.

Most people think success comes from big, one-time efforts (like an intense month of work or an all-nighter). The 1% Rule States: If you improve by just 1% every day, you will be 37 times better in a year. Small, consistent actions create exponential results. I'll share more specific details of this with you here...

- In reality, success is built through tiny, consistent improvements every single day.
- The Math of Compounding:

Formula: $(1.01)^{365} = 37.78$
If you decline by 1% daily, you lose almost all progress: $(0.99)^{365} = 0.03$
The lesson here is that small improvements seem insignificant in the moment, but over time, they create exponential growth.

The Compounding Effect of Habits: Just like investments, tiny daily improvements stack up over time.

- Every habit you build acts like a small deposit into your "success bank."
- At first, the results are invisible, but over time, they snowball into huge gains.

Example:
Writing 500 words per day = a book in 4-6 months.
Reaching out to one potential client per day = 30 connections per month.
Reading 10 pages per day = 12-15 books per year.
The lesson I am sharing with you here is that what seems like "not enough" today becomes life-changing over time.

Success isn't about making huge leaps—it's about consistent micro-wins.

Real-world examples of how consistent daily habits led to massive breakthroughs in business, writing, and marketing.

How to embrace patience—understanding that big success is the result of hundreds of small, seemingly insignificant actions.

Defining Success as an Entrepreneur, Marketer, Content and Course Creator, and/or Writer

Success isn't just about money or followers—it's about progress, consistency, and mastery of your craft. Learn how to set personal success benchmarks based on what truly matters to you.

Avoid the dangers of comparison at all costs: Looking at others' success can destroy your own momentum and drag you down mentally, emotionally, and physically.

Embrace the habit of tracking your progress and believe me when I tell you this is essential for sustaining long-term motivation.

How to create a "success identity"—a mindset shift where you see yourself as a disciplined, consistent creator.

The Success by Design Framework: Build Habits, Reinforce Discipline, and Stay Consistent

Introducing the three pillars of long-term success:

Building the right habits (intentional actions that support your goals).

Reinforcing discipline (creating an environment where good habits thrive).

Staying consistent (showing up every day, even when progress feels slow).

Success by Design: How Smart Entrepreneurs and Creators Build Lasting Habits

How this book will help readers design a system that makes success inevitable.

A preview of upcoming chapters, showing how everything ties together into a structured plan.

Ending with a quick-win challenge: A small, immediate action to start building the reader's success habits today.

The *Success by Design* Framework: Build Habits, Reinforce Discipline, and Stay Consistent

Introducing the three pillars of long-term success:

- Building the right habits (intentional, inspired actions that support your goals).
- Reinforcing discipline (creating an environment where good habits thrive).
- Staying consistent (showing up every day, even when progress feels slow).
- How this book will help you the reader design a system that makes success inevitable.
- A preview of upcoming chapters, showing how everything ties together into a structured plan.
- Ending with a quick-win challenge: A small, immediate action to start building the reader's success habits today.

This first chapter serves as you, the reader's first mindset shift, helping you see that success is not about luck or talent but about what you do consistently every single day. I will encourage you to return to this chapter whenever you feel like you've gotten off track, or when you are returning to reading or listening to it after some time away. Seeing the world through fresh eyes on a regular basis is the gift you give yourself to make your life's journey more sweet and infinitely more satisfying.

Chapter Two

The Science of Habit Formation – How to Rewire Your Brain for Success

"Success isn't about working harder—it's about designing habits that make success inevitable." ~ Unknown

In this chapter, we will dive into the psychology and neuroscience behind habit formation. By understanding how habits work at a biological and psychological level, you can take control of your behaviors and intentionally design habits that lead to success.

Everything is a choice in our life, as we have something called agency

How Habits are Formed: The Habit Loop

In his book *The Power of Habit*, Charles Duhigg explains that every habit follows a three-step loop:

1. **Cue (Trigger)** – A signal that prompts a behavior. (Example: Your phone buzzes.)
2. **Routine (Action)** – The behavior itself. (Example: You check the notification.)
3. **Reward (Benefit)** – A positive reinforcement that makes you want to repeat it. (Example: You get a dopamine hit from reading a message.)

Key Insight:

Success by Design: How Smart Entrepreneurs and Creators Build Lasting Habits

- Habits stick because your brain craves the reward and begins anticipating it. Once a habit is formed, the cue triggers the action automatically, even without conscious thought.

The Role of Dopamine in Habit Formation: Why Some Habits Stick and Some Don't

- Habits form because of dopamine, the brain's "reward chemical."
- When you do something pleasurable (e.g., checking social media, eating sugar), your brain releases dopamine, reinforcing the behavior.
- Over time, the **anticipation of the reward becomes stronger than the reward itself**—this is why cravings drive habits.

How to Use Dopamine to Build Good Habits

- **Make good habits pleasurable** – Attach rewards to productive behaviors (e.g., listening to your favorite music while exercising).
- **Use immediate reinforcement** – Give yourself **small wins** after completing a habit (e.g., checking off a task in a habit tracker).
- **Remove the reward from bad habits** – If you want to break a bad habit, make it **less rewarding** (e.g., making junk food harder to access).

Resource: _Atomic Habits_ by James Clear (Ch. 2: How Your Habits Shape Your Identity)

Neuroplasticity: How to Rewire Your Brain for Success... What is Neuroplasticity?

- Your brain is **not fixed**—it is constantly rewiring itself based on what you do repeatedly.
- The more you repeat an action, the stronger the neural pathways become, making the habit easier over time.
- This is why **good habits become automatic** and bad habits are hard to break.

How to Rewire Your Brain with Repetition

Consistency is key – The more you repeat a behavior, the stronger the neural connections become.
Reduce friction – Make good habits easy to start and bad habits hard to do.
Replace, don't erase – Instead of trying to eliminate bad habits, replace them with better alternatives.

Resource: *The Brain That Changes Itself* by Norman Doidge

How to Make Good Habits Stick: The Four Laws of Behavior Change *(James Clear, Atomic Habits)*

James Clear outlines **four key principles** that make or break a habit.

1. Make it Obvious (Cue)

- Design your environment to **make good habits visible** (e.g., put a book on your pillow to remind you to read).
- Use **implementation intentions**: *"I will [habit] at [time] in [location]."*

2. Make it Attractive (Craving)

- Link good habits to enjoyable things (e.g., pair your morning coffee with writing).

- Surround yourself with people who already have the habit you want.

3. Make it Easy (Action)

- Reduce friction: **Make the habit as easy as possible** (e.g., lay out your workout clothes the night before).
- Follow the **2-Minute Rule** – Start with a tiny version of the habit (e.g., write one sentence instead of committing to an hour).

4. Make it Satisfying (Reward)

- Track progress – Checking off a habit gives a **dopamine boost** that reinforces the behavior.
- Use rewards – Celebrate small wins to keep yourself motivated.

Resource: *Atomic Habits* by James Clear (Ch. 6-9)

Breaking Bad Habits: How to Reverse the Habit Loop

Just as habits are built through repetition, they can be **rewired and replaced**.

The Four Steps to Breaking a Bad Habit

1. **Make it Invisible** – Remove cues (e.g., delete social media apps to stop mindless scrolling).
2. **Make it Unattractive** – Change how you think about the habit (e.g., associate smoking with bad health rather than relaxation).
3. **Make it Difficult** – Add friction (e.g., store your TV remote in another room).
4. **Make it Unsatisfying** – Add accountability (e.g., bet money with a friend that you'll stick to your habit).

Resource: *The Willpower Instinct* by Kelly McGonigal

Habit Stacking: The Shortcut to Building New Habits... What is Habit Stacking?

- Instead of creating habits from scratch, **attach new habits to existing ones**.
- Example:
    - **Current habit:** Drinking coffee in the morning.
    - **New habit:** Write down three priorities while drinking coffee.

Formula: *"After I [current habit], I will [new habit]."*

- *After I brush my teeth, I will meditate for 30 seconds.*
- *After I open my laptop, I will write 50 words.*

Resource: *Atomic Habits* by James Clear (Ch. 5)
Kelly McGonigal

The Golden Rule of Habit Change: Identity Based Habits

Most people fail to change because they focus on outcomes rather than identity.

Outcome-Based vs. Identity-Based Habits

Outcome-Based: "I want to write a book."

Identity-Based: "I am a writer."

Key Shift: Instead of focusing on results, focus on becoming the type of person who does the habit naturally.

Instead of "I need to work out," say "I am an athlete."

Instead of "I need to write," say "I am an author."

Resource: Atomic Habits by James Clear (Ch. 2)

Final Thoughts: Success is a System, Not a One-Time
Decision

The key to rewiring your brain for success is repetition,
environment design, and identity shift. You don't need more
willpower or motivation—you need a structured system that
makes success inevitable.

Key Takeaways from This Chapter:

Habits are built through cues, routines, and rewards.

Dopamine makes habits stick—use it wisely.

Your brain rewires itself based on repetition
(neuroplasticity).

Use habit stacking to make new habits easy.

Shift your identity—act like the person you want to
become.

Section Two

Taking Full Responsibility for Achieving the Level of Success You Desire

"You must take personal responsibility. You cannot change the circumstances, the seasons, or the wind, but you can change yourself. That is something you have charge of." ~ Jim Rohn

Success isn't an accident. It's not a gift handed out to the lucky few. Success is built—brick by brick, habit by habit, choice by choice. And the builders? They are the ones who take full responsibility for where they are now and where they want to go.

This section is about ownership. It's about stepping into the driver's seat of your entrepreneurial journey and realizing that no one else is coming to save you, remind you, or push you forward. Discipline and consistency are the twin forces that separate the dreamers from the doers, the dabblers from the professionals, the wishful thinkers from the success stories.

A Story of Responsibility in Action

Years ago, I met a first-time author who had been "working on a book" for nearly a decade. Every time we spoke, she had a new reason why it wasn't finished: her job was demanding, family life was busy, the timing just wasn't right. Then one day, something changed. She looked me in the eye and said, *"If I don't take responsibility for finishing this, no one else will. This is on me."*

She committed to writing one hour a day, no matter what. Some days the words flowed. Other days they didn't. But she showed up anyway. Within nine months, her manuscript was complete—and within a year, she was holding a published book in her hands.

Her success wasn't the result of sudden inspiration or perfect timing. It was the direct outcome of responsibility, discipline, and consistency.

Discipline is the muscle that keeps you moving when motivation fades. Consistency is the rhythm that turns small actions into unstoppable momentum. Together, they form the backbone of every thriving business, every finished book, every marketing breakthrough.

By the end of this section, you'll see clearly that success is not something you chase—it's something you design, one responsible action at a time. Here is an article that has helped many of the people I mentor, with both their life strategies and their businesses.

Take Full Responsibility for Your Situation to Grow Exponentially

It is impossible to be perfect (whatever that means) all the time. We all make mistakes because we simply cannot always know what the right thing to do is. Admitting that you make mistakes will increase your resilience. Sometimes even powerful leaders are unable or unwilling to admit their mistakes, which weakens their position in the long run. Find the value in your imperfect ways and strive for excellence instead of perfection. It all begins when you take full responsibility for your situation to grow exponentially.

Get curious about the role you play in every part of your life. Even if someone wronged you, get curious about your behavior and reaction. You never have to blame yourself. Simply look at the situation so that you can learn how you want to behave in the future.

As mentioned, there isn't much in this world that you have the power to control. Understanding that fact will provide freedom from a lot of stress.

Just as we have the power to control our reactions to situations, we also have the power to control the next action we take.

If you're able to take a step back and look at a situation objectively, you'll be able to use the information you gain to inform your next steps. It takes humility to look at a situation and see what you could do differently.

Every situation is an opportunity to learn more about yourself. If you can look at yourself while taking a step back to understand with compassion, you'll be able to make wise, well-informed decisions in the future.

Take Ownership of Your Actions

Taking responsibility for your part of your situations can help you take charge of your life. When you're able to look at your life and take a look at your role in it, you can realize your power to overcome.

Begin by getting curious about the situation. For example, if you were fired from your job, you might ask, "Was there anything I could have done differently?" or "What can I learn from this to help me in my next job?"

Remember to have a totally non-judgmental attitude. If you're criticizing yourself, you're not taking responsibility but, instead, digging yourself further into the challenge.

You don't have to think that everything is your fault. Most of the time, it isn't. However, it will strengthen your resilience to take an honest look at your part in your circumstance.

Are there people you need to apologize to?

Sometimes taking ownership for your actions can be difficult. It's important to have humility, especially when you're apologizing to others. Your ability to verbalize your wrongdoings will display your maturity and ability to emotionally regulate.

Resentment can hinder the ability to apologize. If you feel resentment toward anyone, you can take responsibility of your forgiveness process.

Take Full Responsibility and Make Changes

It's difficult to understand exactly how to take responsibility for your own happiness. When things feel out of control and chaotic, it can seem even more difficult. There are a few ways you can really begin to implement changes that will last.

Begin by implementing consistent daily routines. Do the same things each morning that help you get prepared for your day. Include five minutes for a mindfulness exercise.

You can schedule your time in order to help you set boundaries and keep track of your personal growth.

Set reminders to go off throughout the day that will guide you back to the present moment. These reminders can help you to pause in the present moment and move forward from there. Maybe you're in the middle of a crisis and a reminder goes off. This will remind you that you get to make your own decision.

Check in with yourself a few times a day to identify some emotions. By getting in the practice of identifying your emotions, you'll be better able to take responsibility for them and make changes that meet your needs. When you can identify your emotions frequently, you'll be better able to identify them in times of confusion and doubt.

Remember to see every moment as a learning opportunity. Continually ask yourself, "What am I learning from this?" Thinking about this will help you feel more empowered to make changes in your life because it will increase curiosity and self-confidence.

Chapter Three

The Discipline Edge... Staying Committed When Motivation Fades

"Success is never an accident. It is the result of a commitment to excellence, focused effort, consistency, discipline, and intelligent habits." ~ Paul J. Meyer

Discipline is the bridge between intention and achievement. While motivation comes and goes, discipline ensures that your habits continue, your content gets created, your emails get sent, and your goals stay in motion—**even when you don't feel like it**. This chapter is about developing the muscle of discipline and designing a system that doesn't rely on how inspired you feel.

Motivation Is a Spark—Discipline Is the Engine

Motivation is almost exclusively based on emotions. It's often triggered by inspiration, urgency, or a new goal. Discipline is **habitual**. It kicks in **after** motivation fades.

Why Motivation Fails:
- It's **inconsistent** and often **emotion-driven**.
- It's strongest at the **start** of a goal, weakest during the grind.
- It can't withstand distractions, setbacks, or burnout on its own.

Behavioral Insight: According to research from psychologist Dr. BJ Fogg (Stanford), **emotions drive action in the short-term**, but **systems and environment drive long-term behavior.**

Drive by Daniel H. Pink – explores intrinsic vs. extrinsic motivation

Tiny Habits by BJ Fogg – how to build behavior without needing motivation

What Discipline Really Means (And Doesn't Mean)

Discipline is not punishment—it's not about self-denial or grinding through pain.

Discipline is a form of self-leadership. It's about choosing your long-term goals over short-term desires.

Discipline means:

- Creating non-negotiable habits that align with your values
- Keeping promises to yourself
- Following through regardless of emotion
- Working in the dark while trusting the light will come

For creators:

- Writing when you're uninspired
- Launching content when you're afraid it's not perfect
- Finishing the course/product even if you're doubting yourself

Resource:

- **The War of Art by Steven Pressfield – essential reading for understanding resistance and creative discipline**

How to Build the Muscle of Discipline

Discipline is not something you "have"—it's something you train. Like a muscle, it strengthens with use and weakens with neglect.

1. Create Identity-Based Commitments

"I am the type of person who shows up daily."

Discipline flows naturally when it's tied to your identity (e.g., "I am a consistent creator," not "I hope I can stay consistent").

2. Set Process Goals, Not Just Outcome Goals
- Outcome: "Write a bestselling book."
- Process: "Write 500 words every weekday."
  Process goals are within your control, making it easier to stay disciplined.

3. Time-Block & Protect Sacred Hours
- Use time blocking to set up distraction-free zones.
- Treat your work like a meeting with your future self—you wouldn't cancel on them.

4. Use Implementation Intentions
"If it's 8:00 a.m., then I write for 30 minutes."
Clear rules reduce emotional decision-making.

Resources:
- *Deep Work* **by Cal Newport – on working with focus and intention**
- *Atomic Habits* **by James Clear – for pairing identity and consistency**

Designing Systems That Make Discipline Easier

Discipline becomes easier when it's not a battle of willpower every day. Design your life to reduce friction and support your habits.

Key Systems:
- Environmental Design: Keep your tools, templates, and workflow ready. Eliminate distractions before they become problems.
- Accountability: Publicly commit to a schedule or habit (e.g., "I'll publish a blog post every Thursday.")
- Automation: Schedule content, emails, or reminders so that part of your habit runs without thought.
- Tracking Systems: Use habit trackers or apps like Streaks, Notion, or a simple calendar to visually track your discipline.

Resource:
- *The Compound Effect* by Darren Hardy – small, disciplined actions compound into major results over time

What to Do When You Don't Feel Like It

Even the most disciplined people don't always feel like showing up. Here's how they stay consistent anyway:

Strategies:
- The "Just Start" Rule: Commit to just 2 minutes. Often, starting is the hardest part.
- Remove Negotiation: Don't ask yourself "if" you'll do it. Pre-decide.
- Use Rituals: Anchor your discipline with repeatable rituals (e.g., light a candle before writing, play a playlist when creating content).
- Embrace Imperfection: Done is better than perfect. Discipline values momentum over mastery.

Quote:

"You don't rise to the level of your goals. You fall to the level of your systems." – James Clear

Case Studies: Discipline in Action

Example 1: The Consistent Writer

An author commits to writing just 300 words per day. In a year, they have 100,000+ words (1-2 books), all without waiting on motivation.

Example 2: The Email Marketer

A marketer who sends 3 emails per week builds a loyal audience, hones their craft, and creates opportunities, simply because they kept showing up.

Example 3: The Course Creator

Success by Design: How Smart Entrepreneurs and Creators Build Lasting Habits

A creator sets a 90-day challenge: 1 hour of creation per day, no exceptions. At the end, they have a finished course and an audience who watched the journey.

The Mental Game of Discipline

- **Don't chase perfection—chase consistency.**
- **Expect resistance—and plan for it.**
- **Emotionally detach from results—just do the work.**
- **Talk to yourself like a coach, not a critic.**

Resources:
- *Can't Hurt Me* by David Goggins – on building mental toughness
- *Grit* by Angela Duckworth – on passion + perseverance for long-term goals

Final Takeaway: Discipline Is Freedom

While motivation is fleeting, discipline builds freedom. Freedom to create what you want. Freedom to build a business on your terms. Freedom to become the person who follows through.

"At first, discipline feels like a cage. Eventually, it becomes the key to unlock the life you want."

Chapter Four

Consistency Over Perfection: The Key to Long-Term Success

"When you make the right choices — however small — and do it consistently over time, it can make a huge difference in your life. If you remember why you're making those choices, it becomes easier." ~ John C. Maxwell from his book, 'The 15 Invaluable Laws of Growth'

Why Consistency Beats Perfection

- Perfection is a trap. Many new entrepreneurs delay launching a product, blog, or marketing campaign because they want it to be flawless. In reality, perfectionism leads to procrastination.
- Consistency allows you to get in the game, gather feedback, and improve through iteration.
- Example: A writer who commits to writing 500 words a day will complete a book in months. A writer who waits for the "perfect idea" may never start.

The Compound Effect of Showing Up

- Success is not about one perfect effort but about **showing up repeatedly over time.**
- The **"80% Rule"**: It's better to produce consistently at 80% quality than occasionally at 100% (because 100% often never happens).

- In marketing: sending regular emails, posting consistent content, or running steady campaigns builds trust. Irregular "perfect" posts don't.

Consistency Builds Trust and Momentum

- Your audience doesn't expect you to be perfect—they expect you to be **present.**
- **Consistency = Reliability.** Whether it's publishing, marketing, or business habits, being predictable creates loyalty.
- Example: Seth Godin's daily blog isn't perfect every day, but readers trust him because he *shows up daily.*

Practical Ways to Stay Consistent

- **Set Minimum Standards:** Instead of "I'll write 2,000 words," say "I'll write at least 200 words." Small commitments keep you moving.
- **Use Systems, Not Willpower:** Automate or schedule tasks (email sequences, social posts, writing times) to stay on track.
- **Batching:** Group similar tasks together (e.g., writing three blog posts at once) to make consistency easier.
- **Accountability:** Share goals with peers or use tools like habit trackers to stay honest.

Overcoming the Perfectionist's Trap

- Reframe mistakes: **progress over polish.** Each "imperfect attempt" is a stepping stone toward mastery.
- Understand the **80/20 principle**: 80% of your results come from consistent action, not flawless execution.
- Example: An entrepreneur who consistently tests ads learns what works. The perfectionist waits too long and misses opportunities.

Conclusion: The Long Game Wins

- **Consistency creates momentum, momentum creates progress, and progress compounds into success.**
- Perfection may look good on paper, but consistency actually builds a business, a book, or a body of work.
- Final thought: *Don't aim to be perfect tomorrow—aim to show up today.*

Resources to Mention

- *Atomic Habits* by James Clear – for building small, consistent habits.
- *The Practicing Mind* by Thomas M. Sterner – for embracing process over perfection.
- Seth Godin's blog – a model of consistency over decades.

Reader Exercise: The Consistency Challenge

Objective: To prove to yourself that consistency matters more than perfection by committing to a small, repeatable action for 30 days.

Why This Challenge Matters

Perfection may look pretty, but it rarely produces results. Consistency, on the other hand, is the quiet force that builds businesses, books, and brands. Think of this challenge as your training ground. You're not here to prove you can be perfect—you're here to prove you can keep showing up. If you stick with this for 30 days, even imperfectly, you'll discover the momentum and confidence that come only from consistency.

Step 1: Choose Your Area of Focus

Pick one area where consistency will move the needle most for you as a new entrepreneur, marketer, or writer. Examples:
- Writing 200 words a day toward your book or blog.
- Posting on social media 3 times a week.
- Sending one email to your list every week.
- Reading 10 pages of a business or marketing book daily.

Step 2: Define Your Minimum Standard

Instead of aiming for perfection, set the smallest possible action that still builds momentum.
- Example: *"I'll write 200 words a day, even if they're messy."*
- Example: *"I'll post one short tip video every Monday, even if it's not perfectly edited."*

Step 3: Create Your Tracking System

Consistency is easier when you can see your progress.
- Use a calendar and mark an "X" each day you complete your action.
- Try a habit-tracking app like HabitBull, Streaks, or Loop Habit Tracker.
- Keep a simple journal: Write down your daily action and how you felt afterward.

Step 4: Commit to 30 Days

Consistency becomes powerful when it stretches beyond a week. Give yourself 30 days—not to be perfect, but to stay present.
- Miss a day? Don't quit. Restart immediately the next day.

- Remember: *The streak isn't broken until you stop completely.*

Step 5: Reflect and Adjust

At the end of 30 days, review your results:
- How much did your consistency improve?
- What progress did you make, even with imperfect actions?
- What did you learn about yourself?

Your Success Reminder:

Consistency doesn't demand that you be perfect—it asks only that you keep showing up. Over time, showing up creates the kind of success that perfectionists only dream about.

Remember, consistency becomes powerful when it stretches beyond a week. You may have to start over again many times, but it will all be worth it, I promise.

Here is an article on this topic that you may benefit from reading...

When Perfection is Your Goal, You Have a Long Way to Fall

I will preface this essay by sharing that I am a recovering perfectionist. It wasn't until I was almost forty years old that I realized this was the case. Once I did, my life became both easier and more challenging, simultaneously. What came next changed my life and that's what I intend to share with you here.

It was the late fall of 1993 and I was having my final walk through with the social worker before I could be certified as a potential foster parent. She was a pleasant woman named Sheila and a mother of two toddlers of her own. We walked down the hallway leading from my master bedroom back into the living room, and as we turned the corner, I'll never forget what she said.

"You're a perfectionist, Connie. These children will be coming to you from a variety of traumatic situations and highly dysfunctional families and won't be able to meet your standards."

I waited a moment before addressing her comment. It was in a defensive tone I answered "I am not a perfectionist. Just look around, nothing here is perfect."

She smiled politely and changed the subject.

As she backed out of my driveway and drove down the street, I watched until her care was out of sight. I was not happy about what she had said and it hurt me that she didn't allow me to explain and defend myself so she could take it back. So, I turned on the television and sat on the sofa to think about her comment.

Sheila was a licensed social worker (LCSW) who had worked with the Children's Home Society for almost a decade. After graduating with honors from my alma mater, UCLA, she had dedicated her time and focus to volunteering in the community and becoming a foster parent herself. I had no doubt she knew what she was talking about when it came to recognizing personality traits. That is why I turned off the sound on the television and took a small notebook off my shelf to engage in some self-examination.

I made a list of everything I was doing right now that I considered to be perfect. Nothing came up for me so I dug a little deeper. Alright, my closet was perfect. It was a cedar lined, walk in closet that was large enough to serve as a child's bedroom. I had arranged my clothes according to type of item, including shirts, pants, skirts, dresses, sweatshirts, shorts, and so on. Within each group they were lined up by color, size, and season. A year or so ago I had counted how many items I had (98) and purchased hangers in five colors to further arrange everything. When I did the laundry, everything was then hung up to the right, so as not to be worn before the other items within that category unless there was a very good reason.

Yes, this closet with my clothes was perfect. When Vera, another teacher at my school had come to visit it was almost the first thing I showed her. She had smiled her approval and silently moved a pair of jeans to the other side of the closet where they could be with my other jeans instead of next to my blue pants in different shades.

What else was perfect? I walked in and out of every room, including the bedroom where my new foster child would reside. He or she would have the perfect (isn't it alright to use that word) bedroom, decorated in a pale shade of green so as to be perfect for either a boy or a girl. There were bunk beds with a tiny ladder, and a desk that pulled out from the side. This would be perfect if siblings arrived at my door.

I sat back down in front of the muted television. Suddenly I didn't feel so good. I strode into the kitchen, holding my head and thinking about making a grilled cheese sandwich. No, I couldn't. I didn't have the right cheese. And my sourdough bread was going stale. Perhaps I could run to the market and get what I needed quickly so I could come home and make the, you guessed it, the perfect grilled cheese sandwich.

But these were just words. I wasn't striving for perfection all the time. When perfection is your goal, you think about it all the time so it can be your reality. I wasn't doing that. I just liked certain things to be done in a particular way. Did I expect this from others?

The images were beginning to irritate me, so I used the remote to turn off the television. As I placed the remote back into its holder, I went into slow motion to observe my own behavior. My life began to flash in front of my eyes as I finally came to terms with what had been going on in my life for decades. Here I was, almost forty and still believing that everything and everyone had to be perfect in order to succeed. One misstep and everything goes awry. When perfection is your goal, you have a long way to fall.

And fall I had. My life was a mess. Other people were to blame, in my way of thinking. It began with my parents, then my so-called friends, and finally, the people I worked with. Then I carried it over to inanimate objects and physical possessions. I thought back to the leather chair I had spent almost a month's pay on, only to get it home and find that the leather on the backrest was filled with imperfections. The man at the store had practically laughed out loud when I called to complain. "You want it perfect, buy something man made. Nature doesn't create with perfection as a goal." I had hung up the phone, attempting to slam down the receiver so he would know my displeasure.

I thought next to the relationships I had irreparably damaged, beginning with the one I had with my mother. All this time I had believed that she wanted me to be perfect in every way, but that didn't seem to be the case upon closer examination. She wanted me to be happy, and that's quite a different thing altogether. The piano and voice lessons were the prime example. She had accepted nothing less than perfection when I practiced, but only so I could move past the "unconscious incompetence" stage and forward towards "unconscious competence" at some point in the future. But the future never came because I had quit trying and blamed her for ruining my life in the 3rd grade by taking me away from my friends. She hadn't understood when I cried and told her my friends were the most important people in my life and they didn't care if I could sing or play the piano or anything else because they liked me the way I was. And I didn't understand when those friends went away, one by one and over time, to the point that I can't even remember but a few of their names, all these years later.

In Kindergarten a boy and I had climbed over the fence at recess, while the teachers were on a smoke break and not watching, and made it the two long blocks to see a sunflower in someone's yard. That flower was so beautiful and so imperfect. That made it unique, a word I had not heard at that time but most certainly knew the meaning of in a special way. The sunflower was only interesting and worth escaping from the schoolyard to see because it was a one of kind creation of Nature. If this is true, then imperfection is the only perfection, it seems.

And this leads me to the point of this essay, which is to share with you how I was able to finally overcome my perfectionist tendencies and get back on track with my life...

As I was leaving my previous life as a classroom teacher and real estate broker and residential appraiser behind at the end of 2005, in favor of coming online as an entrepreneur, something occurred that shook me to my core. My childhood friend, Tory, was going through a difficult time in his life and reached out to me for support. Tory had struggled to overcome a strict father who refused to settle for anything less than perfection from his four children. He dished out verbal and physical abuse on a regular basis. My family lived next door to them for three years while I was in junior high and I observed much of this firsthand.

Tory was a special person. He was funny and creative and well-liked by everyone. By high school he shared with me that he was gay, and I was not surprised by this announcement. Of course, his goal became to make sure his father would never find out and he worked diligently to keep this part of his life a secret. But he remained focused on perfection and insisted that everything he attempted be done "right" as he referred to it. Seldom were his efforts close to perfect, and this kept him from reaching anything close to his full potential over the thirty-eight years we were close friends.

The day before Christmas in 2005 I received a call from his mother that Tory had passed away unexpectedly. He had moved back in with her after his father died the year before. On that afternoon he had gone to the store to pick up some last-minute items for the Christmas Day dinner he would prepare for the family members that would be arriving the following day. We had spoken on the phone and he told me he wanted everything to be perfect for this first Christmas without his father.

He bought a sandwich from the deli and sat down on a bench, in the park where we had played as children, to eat it before heading home. The paramedics arrived just before midnight and pronounced him dead at the scene. He had choked on the sandwich and no one had been around to help. It was a lady walking her dog who saw him lying on the ground and called the police.

I loved Tory like a brother. He and I visited so many places and had many adventures over the years. His passing hit me hard and on Christmas Day I took on the task of calling people all over the world to let them know what had happened to our sweet friend. Whenever I think about how perfectionism can keep someone from achieving their life dreams, it is Tory's shortened life that comes to mind. On that fateful day I made a promise to myself to never again set the goal of perfection with anything I would take on, personally or in my business. When perfection is your goal, you have a long way to fall.

This is from "*All of Me*" by John Legend...

'Cause all of me
Loves all of you
Love your curves and all your edges
All your perfect imperfections
Give your all to me
I'll give my all to you
You're my end and my beginnin'
Even when I lose, I'm winnin'.

I've come to realize that I am a human forever in training, and filled with perfect imperfections. It's the consistency of what we do each and every day that truly makes the difference.

"Progress beats perfection every time and consistency is choosing progress over perfection, every single day. Your small

steps taken consistently lead to giant leaps in results." ~ Connie Ragen Green

Section Three
Building Keystone Habits for Business and Creativity

"Do not let what you cannot do interfere with what you can do. Keystone habits will make the difference." ~ John Wooden

Not all habits are created equal. Some habits move the needle more than others—these are your **keystone habits.** Just as the keystone in an arch holds the entire structure together, keystone habits create ripple effects that strengthen everything else in your business and creative life.

When you identify and cultivate these high-leverage habits, success begins to feel less like an uphill battle and more like a natural progression. For entrepreneurs, that might mean setting a habit of planning the day before it starts, which leads to sharper focus, better decisions, and more consistent sales. For writers, it could be the habit of writing 500 words daily, which not only builds a book but also builds confidence and momentum.

The beauty of keystone habits is their power to compound. One habit can spill over into improved health, sharper focus, deeper relationships, and increased creativity. When you focus on the right keystone habits, you're not just improving one area—you're designing a foundation that supports all of them.

In this section, we'll uncover which habits have the power to transform your business and your creative work, and how to install them into your daily life. By the end, you'll not only know what keystone habits to prioritize—you'll have a system for making them stick.

You may need to think this idea over for a while, and allow what I am sharing with you here to ruminate for a few days. This will be time well spent, I promise.

A Story of Transformation Through a Keystone Habit

When Maya, a freelance copywriter, came to me for guidance, she was drowning in half-finished projects, missed deadlines, and constant stress. Her problem wasn't talent—she was brilliant with words. Her problem was chaos. Every day, she started work by diving into emails, reacting to messages, and chasing client requests. By noon, she was drained, and the writing—the one thing that could actually grow her business— was left undone.

I suggested a simple keystone habit: plan tomorrow, today. Each evening, she spent 10 minutes outlining her top three priorities for the next day, with writing always first.

Within a month, everything shifted. She was consistently writing every morning, which meant projects got finished ahead of schedule. With her afternoons freed up for client calls and marketing, she landed two new long-term contracts. The ripple effects extended beyond business—she felt calmer, more confident, and even had the energy to start exercising again.

Maya didn't overhaul her entire life. She installed one keystone habit, and it transformed her work, her business, and her mindset.

Here are four keystone habits tailored for entrepreneurs, marketers, and writers — each one creates a ripple effect that strengthens other areas of life and business.

1. Daily Planning and Reflection
- *Why it's a keystone:* Spending 10 minutes each evening to plan the next day reduces decision fatigue, increases

productivity, and keeps you aligned with your bigger goals.
- *Ripple effect:* Clear priorities → less procrastination → more consistent progress → increased confidence.

2. Consistent Content Creation
- *Why it's a keystone:* For writers and marketers, creating daily (even in small amounts) builds an "output mindset" instead of waiting for inspiration.
- *Ripple effect:* Improves writing skills → builds authority → creates marketing assets → generates long-term visibility and income.

3. Morning Movement or Mindfulness
- *Why it's a keystone:* Starting the day with exercise, stretching, or meditation primes your energy, focus, and creativity.
- *Ripple effect:* Better health → sharper focus → lower stress → more resilience in handling setbacks.

4. Tracking Key Metrics
- *Why it's a keystone:* Measuring what matters (sales, leads, writing word count, or habits completed) creates clarity and accountability.
- *Ripple effect:* Awareness → better decisions → faster course corrections → steady growth over time.

Keystone Habit Discovery Exercise

Step 1: Reflect on What's Working (and What's Not)

Ask yourself:
- Which parts of my business or creative work feel the most stressful or chaotic right now?
- Where do I lose the most time or energy?

- What's one area where small, consistent improvement could make everything else easier?

Write down your thoughts.

Step 2: Spot the Leverage Points

Think of habits that could:
- Eliminate daily friction (like planning ahead).
- Create output that compounds (like consistent writing or content creation).
- Improve your energy and focus (like movement or mindfulness).
- Give you clarity and accountability (like tracking key metrics).

Circle the 1–2 that stand out most for you.

Step 3: Choose One Keystone Habit

Pick the single habit that feels like it would create the biggest ripple effect in your life and business. Don't worry about doing everything—start with one.

Write it here:

My keystone habit will be: _____

Step 4: Define the First Version

Decide what the smallest, simplest version of this habit looks like:
- 10 minutes of evening planning
- 500 words a day
- 15 minutes of morning movement
- A Friday review of 3 key numbers

Keep it doable.

Step 5: Commit Out Loud

Success by Design: How Smart Entrepreneurs and Creators Build Lasting Habits

Write this affirmation and say it to yourself:
"By focusing on this one habit, I am creating momentum and designing success in my business and life."

Pro Tip: Track your habit for the next 30 days. Each time you check it off, you're not just completing a task—you're strengthening your identity as a disciplined entrepreneur and creator.

Perhaps this article will give you a new perspective in this area...

Habits or Routines... Which Do You Need?

As I am writing this blog post it is Wednesday, October 30th, in the year 2024 and there are only 61 days remaining in this year. This got me to thinking about how we can all be a lot more intentional and productive in our life and for our business, and in ways that will make a difference for us and for those around us. Are you developing habits or routines that will benefit you now and over time?

Where are you going and where have you been?

Are you creating a schedule for each day, based on your to-do list from the previous day? Our to-do lists can be a mile long and make us feel that we aren't accomplishing very much each day. But on closer examination, you will most likely discover that you did tackle and complete, or at least make progress on the one or two items of greatest importance on yesterdays to do this.

So no, this is what I want you to do...

Take a look at your to-do list from today. Think of each item on this list and decide if it is something you no longer wish or need to do, if it is something that can be delegated to someone else to do, if it can be postponed until a later date, or if it is something you must do yourself today.

The goal is to choose no more than four items for today and then move these things from your to-do list over to today's schedule. I combine personal and business tasks and activities, so for today my schedule consists of writing an email message to send to my list of subscribers, answering an email from someone I am an affiliate for, and accompanying a family member to a doctor's appointment.

I do not include things like brushing my teeth, turning on my computer, or refilling my water bottle, as these are things that have become habits, even though they are a part of my morning routine.

Now, I want you to think about the difference, in your mind, between habits and routines. I have a writing routine I use for my blog posts, and a different routine for the movie script I am currently working on. The routine I have recently created for writing and publishing blog posts is one that I hope to soon turn into a habit, while my script writing routine will most likely remain as a routine until I become more confident with this style of writing.

What are your goals for the next 30 days? Write them down and then look to see if you will need both a routine and habits to make these tasks and activities come to fruition. The answer depends upon what you have been doing on a daily or regular basis in each of these areas.

For example, beginning in 2020 I got into the habit of eating with a focus on intermittent fasting. I did not have to think each morning about what I was going to eat because I already knew the period of time I would be eating and exactly what I was going to eat that day.

Success by Design: How Smart Entrepreneurs and Creators Build Lasting Habits

At the beginning of 2024, I let my intermittent fasting practice go, and with it the powerful and effective habits I had cemented in my thinking during those previous four years.

Now I have gone back to intermittent fasting as a way of life, so I needed to create a new routine that would work well for me. Because I had done this four years ago, there was some "muscle memory" that kicked in, but it was still like starting at the very beginning. In some ways, I am grateful for this fresh start. I am choosing the foods I eat and the time of day I will be eating them with the knowledge I did not possess years ago.

And now, I'll share with you an example from my business. Over the past fifteen years or so, I have created more than fifty products and courses to teach and sell in my business. At some point, I stopped creating anything new and simply began teaching new "seasons" of my most popular courses so that the people who had purchased them years earlier would continue to be included in the new information I was teaching.

Now that I am ready to begin creating new courses and products, but they will be different from what I have done before. Why? Because I have new knowledge and experience as to what is most appealing to today's audiences, as well as with what brings me to most joy and satisfaction.
~ Connie Ragen Green

Chapter Five
Eliminating Distractions: How to Focus in a Noisy World

"This has been one of my mantras - focus and simplicity.
Simple can be harder than complex: You have to work hard to
get your thinking clean to make it simple. But it's worth it in the
end because once you get there, you can move mountains."
~ Steve Jobs.

The Cost of Distraction

- **Attention is currency.** Every distraction you entertain costs you momentum, creativity, and results.
- Studies show it takes **23 minutes and 15 seconds** on average to regain focus after an interruption.
- Distractions are not just lost time—they're lost opportunities to move your business, book, or brand forward.
- Example: An entrepreneur who checks email every 10 minutes is "working," but not producing meaningful results.

The Entrepreneur's Distraction Traps

- **Digital distractions:** Constant notifications, endless scrolling, checking analytics obsessively.
- **Workplace distractions:** Multitasking, cluttered desk, saying yes to too many meetings.
- **Internal distractions:** Procrastination, self-doubt, shiny object syndrome, mental chatter.

- For newer entrepreneurs and marketers, the biggest distraction often comes disguised as **"research" or "preparation"**—but really, it's avoidance.

The Myth of Multitasking

- Multitasking feels productive but actually reduces efficiency and increases errors.
- **Switching costs**: Every time you switch between writing, marketing, and checking social media, your brain spends energy re-orienting.
- Focus is a **superpower** in today's noisy world. The most successful entrepreneurs are those who protect it fiercely.

Designing a Focus-Friendly Environment

- **Digital hygiene:**
  - Turn off non-essential notifications.
  - Use tools like Freedom, Cold Turkey, or StayFocusd to block distractions.
  - Schedule email and social media checks instead of reacting instantly.
- **Physical environment:**
  - Declutter your workspace to reduce decision fatigue.
  - Create a dedicated work area to signal your brain "this is focus time."
- **Rituals for focus:**
  - Use cues (music, a candle, a specific desk setup) to trigger deep work.
  - Try the **Pomodoro Technique** (25 minutes on, 5 minutes off).

Mastering Your Attention

- **Single-tasking > multitasking.** Work in clear blocks of time on one priority.
- **Time blocking:** Schedule your most important work during your peak energy hours.
- **Attention audits:** Track where your time and focus actually go for one week—you'll spot hidden drains on productivity.
- **Deep work sessions:** Set aside distraction-free time for your most valuable tasks (like writing, creating, or strategic planning).

Managing Internal Distractions

- **Shiny Object Syndrome:** Remind yourself, *"Not now— later."* Keep a "parking lot list" for ideas so they don't derail your current work.
- **Mindfulness practices:** Breathing exercises, journaling, or meditation to calm the mental noise.
- **Clarity of goals:** Distractions lose their grip when you're crystal clear on what matters most.

Stories and Case Studies

- **Entrepreneur Example:** A new marketer I began working with recently limited social media use to two 15-minute blocks a day and gained back 10+ hours weekly to grow her business.
- **Writer Example:** J.K. Rowling rented a hotel room to finish *Harry Potter*—removing all home distractions.
- **Personal productivity example:** Warren Buffett attributes his success to the ability to say "no" to almost everything that isn't his top priority.

Action Steps for You, the Reader

- Conduct a **Distraction Audit**: Track interruptions for one week. Identify your biggest time-wasters.
- Choose **one digital distraction** to eliminate or reduce (e.g., turn off phone alerts).
- Choose **one focus ritual** to implement (e.g., morning writing block, Pomodoro, workspace declutter).
- Practice saying **"no"** to commitments that don't align with your goals.

Conclusion: Focus Is Freedom

- Focus is the modern entrepreneur's unfair advantage.
- By eliminating distractions, you buy back your time, energy, and creativity.
- Final thought: *You don't need more hours in the day— you need fewer distractions in the hours you already have.*

Resources to Mention

- *Deep Work* by Cal Newport – on the power of focused work in a distracted world.
- *Indistractable* by Nir Eyal – on mastering internal and external distractions.
- *Essentialism* by Greg McKeown – on focusing only on what truly matters.

Reader Exercise The "Distraction Detox Challenge"

The Modern Focus Crisis

- We live in the noisiest era in human history: smartphones, social media, endless notifications, and an expectation of instant replies.

- For entrepreneurs and writers, this means attention is constantly under siege. The very tools that help you run your business — email, marketing platforms, social channels — are also the ones that distract you most.
- Neuroscience shows that every distraction (checking a message, toggling between tasks, scrolling feeds) comes with a switching cost. It can take up to 23 minutes to fully refocus after a single interruption.

Why Distraction Destroys Progress

- Distractions fragment your time and energy, preventing deep work — the type of sustained concentration where true creativity and problem-solving thrive.
- Small, constant interruptions add up to hours of lost productivity each week.
- Worse, they train your brain to crave shallow stimulation instead of discipline and focus. Over time, this erodes your ability to stay committed to meaningful tasks.

Strategies for Eliminating Distractions

1. **Create a Controlled Environment**
   - Design a workspace that minimizes visual and digital noise.
   - Simple changes (closing tabs, silencing notifications, using noise-canceling headphones) create powerful results.
2. **Set Boundaries with Technology**
   - Use tools like *Freedom*, *Cold Turkey Blocker*, or your phone's "Focus Mode" to limit distracting apps and websites during work hours.
   - Entrepreneurs can set "office hours" for email and social media instead of letting them run the day.
3. **Master the Single Task Rule**

- Multitasking is a myth — research shows it reduces efficiency and increases mistakes.
- Commit to "uni-tasking" — completing one focused block of work before moving to the next.

4. **Leverage the Power of Rituals**
   - Create a pre-focus ritual to signal to your brain: *it's time to work.*
   - This could be brewing tea, lighting a candle, or opening a specific notebook. Consistent cues train your mind to enter a flow state faster.

5. **Guard Your Energy, Not Just Your Time**
   - Distraction isn't always external — sometimes it's fatigue, stress, or lack of clarity.
   - Prioritize sleep, healthy routines, and clear daily priorities to reduce internal distractions.

The Entrepreneur's Edge

- Marketers and writers who learn to manage distractions don't just get more done — they produce higher-quality work.
- Focused time allows for better copywriting, more compelling storytelling, stronger marketing campaigns, and innovative product ideas.
- In a world where attention is fragmented, **the ability to focus becomes a competitive advantage**.

Practical Focus Framework

1. **Morning Power Hour** → Start the day with 60–90 minutes of distraction-free, high-value work.
2. **Digital Detox Blocks** → Schedule at least two blocks daily with no devices.
3. **End-of-Day Reset** → Clean workspace, close tabs, write tomorrow's top 3 tasks.

Success by Design: How Smart Entrepreneurs and Creators Build Lasting Habits

Resources & Tools

- **Books**:
  - *Deep Work* by Cal Newport
  - *Indistractable* by Nir Eyal
- **Apps**:
  - Forest (gamifies focus with tree growth)
  - Freedom (blocks apps/sites)
  - Todoist or ClickUp (task management)
- **Methods**:
  - Pomodoro Technique (25-minute focus sprints)
  - Time-blocking calendar

Key Takeaway: Distractions are the enemy of habits, discipline, and consistency. By reclaiming focus in a noisy world, entrepreneurs and writers unlock their deepest creative potential and accelerate their path to success.

Chapter Six
Designing a Habit System for Success

"The difference between an amateur and a professional is in their habits. An amateur has amateur habits, while a professional has professional habits. We can never free ourselves from habit. But we can replace bad habits that don't serve us with good ones that do." ~ Steven Pressfield

Most entrepreneurs and creators fail not because they lack ambition, but because they rely on scattered habits instead of a system. One good habit here, another good habit there—it's progress, but it's fragile. Without structure, habits can easily collapse under pressure.

This is a pivotal chapter because it moves you from individual habits (like I covered in Section Three) into a system of habits that work together to support your bigger vision.

Here, I'll show you how to design a habit ecosystem—a set of routines, triggers, and environments that support each other and make success almost automatic.

Why Systems Beat Goals

- Goals set direction, but systems drive progress.
- Example: The goal might be "write a book," but the system is "write 500 words every morning, outline each week, revise every Friday."
- Systems make success sustainable because they remove decision fatigue—you don't have to ask *what* to do each day; you just follow the system.

Resource: James Clear, *Atomic Habits* → "You do not rise to the level of your goals. You fall to the level of your systems."

Building a Habit Ecosystem

- Habits don't exist in isolation; they reinforce one another.
- Example: A morning movement habit fuels energy → energy supports writing → writing builds authority → authority grows business.
- Teach readers to stack habits so one action triggers the next (habit stacking).

Exercise: List three current habits, then brainstorm ways to "stack" new habits onto them (e.g., after brewing coffee → write 100 words).

Designing Routines That Stick

- Morning routines for focus and creativity.
- Workday startup and shutdown rituals.
- Evening routines for reflection and planning.
- Show readers how routines anchor keystone habits into a rhythm that builds momentum.

Anecdote: Benjamin Franklin's daily schedule as an early example of routine design.

Environment as Invisible System

- Your surroundings either make habits easier or harder.
- Example: If your phone is on the desk, distraction is one click away. If your writing notebook is open on the desk, writing is frictionless.
- Teach readers to audit their environment for friction vs. flow.

Tool: Create a "Habit Environment Map"—list cues in your workspace that push you toward focus vs. distraction.

Automating Success

- Systems are strongest when they remove choice.
- Examples:
    - Automating savings/investing for financial habits.
    - Scheduling focus blocks into calendar apps.
    - Prepping content outlines at the start of the week.
- Teach readers to let automation and pre-decision carry the weight so willpower doesn't have to.

Conclusion: From Habits to Lifestyle

A single habit can change your day. A habit system can change your life. When you design systems, you're not just reacting—you're building an operating manual for success that runs even when motivation is low.

Mantra: "I don't chase success; I design systems that deliver it."

Connie Ragen Green

Chapter Seven
Success on Autopilot –
Automating Discipline and
Productivity

" Professionals know that discipline and productivity are crucial to success. Amateurs sit and wait for inspiration, the rest of us just get up from in front of the television and get to work."
~ Stephen King

This chapter is where you will really feel the payoff of everything you've learned so far.

The goal of this chapter is to help you transition from *willpower-heavy effort* to *system-powered ease.* By this stage, you've built discipline, consistency, and keystone habits. Now it's about shifting those habits into the background, making them so automatic that success becomes the natural byproduct of daily life—like brushing your teeth.

From Effort to Ease
- In the beginning, success feels like a grind—showing up, resisting distractions, and battling procrastination.
- Once a habit is wired into the brain's basal ganglia, it runs subconsciously. This frees up mental energy for creativity, strategy, and growth.
- Example: Instead of struggling every day to "find time" to write, a writer who builds a morning writing ritual no longer negotiates—it just *happens.*

Systematizing Routine Tasks

- Productivity skyrockets when you build systems that take the thinking out of your day.
- Entrepreneurs can automate:
  - **Marketing:** scheduling emails and social media posts.
  - **Finances:** automated savings, bill payments, or profit transfers.
  - **Learning:** batching podcast listening or setting aside weekly "education hours."
- These systems create consistency without requiring constant decision-making.

The Habit Loop Refined

- Cue → Routine → Reward. By designing intentional loops, you can condition your brain to crave productivity.
- Example: Light a candle and make tea before sitting down to work. Your brain associates this cue with "focus time," so productivity flows more naturally.

Leveraging Technology Wisely

- Technology can either be the greatest ally or the worst distraction. Here, readers learn how to harness apps, timers, and automation tools without becoming dependent or overwhelmed.
- Suggestions:
  - Focus apps like **Forest** or **Freedom** (distraction blockers).
  - Automation tools like **Zapier**, **IFTTT**, or email sequences.
  - Scheduling platforms like **Buffer**, **Later**, or **ConvertKit.**

The Compound Effect of Automation

- When habits are automated, they multiply impact over months and years.

Success by Design: How Smart Entrepreneurs and Creators Build Lasting Habits

- A small daily action (e.g., writing 300 words, posting one piece of content, saving $10) compounds into massive results.
- The key is designing your environment and systems so these habits fire off with minimal resistance.

The Identity Shift: From Forcing to Flowing

- This is where new entrepreneurs and creators shift identities: from "someone who tries to be disciplined" → "someone who is naturally productive."
- Example: Instead of saying, "I'm trying to become consistent with blogging," you evolve into, "I'm a blogger who publishes every week."

Practical Strategies for Readers

- **Create Routines Around Keystone Habits:**
  Build one or two anchor routines (like morning journaling or evening planning) that trigger other habits.
- **Batch and Automate Low-Value Tasks:**
  Spend focused blocks of time creating content, scheduling marketing, or pre-planning. Let automation do the heavy lifting so you can focus on strategy.
- **Use Environment Design:**
  Set up your workspace, digital tools, and calendar to make good habits the *default option*. (E.g., put your gym shoes by the door, or keep your to-do app as your phone's home screen.)
- **Audit Your Energy & Attention:**
  Notice where you waste the most mental bandwidth. Automate or eliminate those areas. (Ex: auto-pay bills, unsubscribe from distracting newsletters, set recurring reminders.)
- **Weekly "Autopilot Check-In":**
  Even though habits run automatically, a weekly review

ensures they're still aligned with your bigger goals and not slipping into complacency.

Resources for Further Reading

- **James Clear, *Atomic Habits*** – Practical frameworks for making habits stick.
- **Charles Duhigg, *The Power of Habit*** – Classic exploration of the habit loop.
- **Cal Newport, *Deep Work*** – Focus and productivity strategies.
- **David Allen, *Getting Things Done*** – Workflow and automation principles.

My Chapter 7 Promise to you, the Reader:

By the end of this chapter, readers will understand how to design their lives and businesses so that the *hard parts of success become automatic.* They'll move from grinding it out to flowing with discipline, where productivity requires less force and more design.

Section Four
Practical Steps to Design a Habit System

"Productivity is never an accident. It is always the result of a commitment to excellence, intelligent planning, and focused effort. This is best accomplished with a system for your habits" ~ Paul J. Meyer

You've already discovered that success isn't built on luck, timing, or endless bursts of motivation—it's built on design. Up to this point, we've explored how your brain forms habits, why discipline always outperforms willpower, and how consistency becomes your most reliable business partner.

Now it's time to build your system.

This section is where everything you've learned so far comes together. It's where you'll move from thinking about success to engineering it—step by step, habit by habit.

As a new entrepreneur or marketer, you don't need more information; you need integration. The right system helps you wake up each morning knowing exactly what matters most, what to do next, and how those actions connect to your long-term goals.

In the next few chapters, we'll create that framework together. You'll identify the keystone habits that make the biggest difference, automate your daily discipline so it feels effortless, and finally pull all the pieces into your Success by Design Blueprint—your personal roadmap for growth, freedom, and fulfillment.

By the time you finish this section, you'll have transformed your habits into an invisible engine—one that runs quietly in the background, fueling your progress every single day.

Because success doesn't come from working harder. It comes from designing smarter.

Where Vision Becomes Action and Action Becomes Success

"Dreams set the destination. Habits pave the road." – *Connie Ragen Green*

This Section is where theory transforms into action. As a newer entrepreneur, marketer, and/or writer, you will move from *understanding* habits to *engineering* them with clarity, structure, and purpose.

Up to this point in the book, you've explored the psychology of success: how habits form, why discipline outlasts motivation, and the power of consistency. Now, it's time to put all of that into practice.

In this section, we'll shift from the *why* to the *how*. You'll learn to build a personal habit system that supports your goals, aligns with your values, and creates daily momentum. This isn't about adding more to your to-do list—it's about creating a rhythm that carries you forward automatically, even when life gets busy.

Whether you're launching your first online business, growing your creative career, or refining your marketing routines, these chapters will help you design habits that *stick*— and systems that make success sustainable.

These chapter will help you:
- Identify keystone habits that deliver maximum results.
- Map habits to their bigger goals (business, marketing, writing, and mindset).
- Create "habit stacks" — linking new actions to existing routines.
- Build systems for tracking progress without burnout.

- Replace old, limiting habits with growth-driven behaviors.

Key Takeaway: Success is not the result of one powerful decision—it's the compound effect of daily, intentional action.

Motivational Quote: "You don't rise to the level of your goals; you fall to the level of your systems." – *James Clear*

Chapter Eight is the culmination of everything in the book. Readers will:

- Integrate habits, systems, and mindset into one cohesive plan.
- Create their personalized *Success by Design Blueprint* (using your fillable worksheet).
- Define milestones, review checkpoints, and reflection practices.
- Plan for growth, scaling, and sustainability in their entrepreneurial journey.

Key Takeaway: A well-designed system frees your mind to focus on creativity, connection, and contribution.

Motivational Quote: "Your habits create your future long before you realize they have already changed your life." ~ *Connie Ragen Green*

Chapter Eight

The Success by Design Blueprint: Putting It All Together

"All theory is gray, but the golden tree of life springs ever green." ~ Johann Wolfgang von Goethe

This Fourth Section is where theory transforms into action. As a newer entrepreneur, marketer, and/or writer, you will move from *understanding* habits to *engineering* them with clarity, structure, and purpose.

Introduction – The Big Picture

By now, readers have learned the core pillars:
- **Habits** as the foundation of success.
- **Discipline** as the engine when motivation fades.
- **Consistency** as the multiplier over time.
- **Systems & automation** as the ultimate design that removes resistance.

But information without structure can still feel overwhelming. This final chapter delivers the **Success by Design Blueprint** — a step-by-step framework to turn these principles into daily, repeatable action.

The Four Pillars of Success by Design

Reinforce the key pillars you've introduced throughout the book, now framed as a connected system:

1. **Habits:** Small actions that form identity.
2. **Discipline:** Staying committed when it's inconvenient.
3. **Consistency:** Showing up long enough to reap compounding results.
4. **Systems:** Creating autopilot success through structure and environment.

Visual: A pyramid or flow chart where habits form the base, discipline strengthens the middle, consistency holds it together, and systems sit at the top as the crown.

The Blueprint Framework – A Practical Path Forward
Offer a **step-by-step method** readers can follow to design their own path:
Step 1: Define Your Identity & Vision
- Who do you want to become? (Writer, entrepreneur, creator?)
- What does success *look like* daily, not just in the future?

Step 2: Identify Keystone Habits
- Choose 2–3 habits with the biggest ripple effect.
- Example: Morning writing (for authors), content batching (for marketers), financial tracking (for entrepreneurs).

Step 3: Build Routines & Environment
- Morning ritual, workday structure, evening wind-down.
- Adjust environment: remove friction, add triggers.

Step 4: Automate Discipline
- Use tools (schedulers, templates, reminders).
- Pre-decide routines (no daily debating what to do).

Step 5: Track & Celebrate Consistency
- Use a simple tracker (calendar checkmarks, habit apps, journal).
- Celebrate progress, not perfection — highlight streaks.

Step 6: Refine & Scale
- Evaluate monthly: What worked? What didn't?

- Eliminate or adjust habits that don't serve your vision.

Common Roadblocks & How to Overcome Them

- **"I lose motivation."** → Replace with pre-set routines; motivation is optional.
- **"I keep slipping."** → Focus on consistency over perfection; missing one day isn't failure.
- **"I get distracted."** → Revisit environment design and distraction management.
- **"I feel overwhelmed."** → Start with *one keystone habit*; layer the rest later.

A Day in the Life of Success by Design

Paint a vivid picture:
- Wake up → follow morning ritual (movement, journaling, writing).
- Work block → focus on priority tasks with no distractions.
- Midday → batch admin tasks.
- Afternoon → creative work or marketing, guided by system, not mood.
- Evening → reflect, review, and prepare for tomorrow.

☞ Show how this "designed day" makes success inevitable without constant strain.

The Legacy of Habits – Why This Matters

Bring emotional weight:
- This isn't just about getting more done — it's about **freedom**.
- Entrepreneurs and writers who design their success systems create space for creativity, family, and impact.
- Small actions compound not only into business growth but into a life that feels intentional and fulfilling.

Conclusion – The Next Step

"Your life and business are being shaped right now by the habits you choose and the systems you design. The question is not whether you have habits — it's whether you've chosen the right ones. With discipline, consistency, and a blueprint built on purpose, success is no longer a gamble. It's by design."

Your Call to Action:

- I Encourage you to build your own **Success by Design Blueprint** (You Could create a printable worksheet or companion resource).
- I invite you to commit to 30 days of small, consistent action.

The Success by Design Blueprint

How Smart Entrepreneurs and Creators Build Lasting Habits That Serve Their Goals and Dreams

Step 1: Define Your Identity & Vision

You can't build habits for someone you don't believe you are.

Prompts:
- Who do I want to become in the next 12 months? (Example: A consistent content creator, a disciplined entrepreneur, a confident writer.)
- What does my *ideal day* look like when I'm living that identity?
- Why does this matter to me — what's at stake if I don't change?

Write your identity statement:
"I am a ___ who ___ every day to create ___."
(Example: I am a writer who shows up daily to create words that inspire and sell.)

Step 2: Choose Your Keystone Habits

Small hinges swing big doors.

Pick 2–3 high-impact habits that will create a ripple effect across your business and life:

1. _____
2. _____
3. _____

Examples:

- Write 500 words each morning.
- Engage with your email list daily.
- Plan tomorrow's priorities each evening.

Trigger these habits with cues:

(After I _____, I will _____.)

Example: After I pour my morning coffee, I'll write my daily email.

Step 3: Build Supportive Routines & Environments

Make the right action the easy action.

Morning Routine:

_____

Workday Start Ritual:

_____

Evening Reflection Ritual:

_____

Environment Audit:

What in my workspace helps me focus?

_____

What consistently distracts me?

_____

What can I change today to make good habits frictionless?

_____

Step 4: Automate Discipline

Don't depend on willpower — design your workflow.
Tools & Automations to Implement:
☐ Email sequences / autoresponders
☐ Content scheduling tools (Buffer, Later, or Metricool)
☐ Calendar blocking
☐ Templates and checklists for repeat tasks
☐ Habit tracker app or wall calendar
Question:
What can I automate this week so it happens without me thinking about it?

Step 5: Track, Reflect & Refine
You can't improve what you don't measure.
Daily:
- ☐ Did I complete my keystone habits?
- ☐ Did I protect my focus time?
- ☐ Did I celebrate small wins?

Weekly Reflection Prompts:
- What went well this week?
- What felt hard or draining?
- What small adjustment could make next week easier?

Monthly Reset:
- Which habits are serving my goals?
- Which habits need to evolve or be replaced?

Step 6: Stay Consistent – Not Perfect
Perfection is the enemy of progress; consistency compounds results.

Miss a day? Don't restart — just continue.
Track streaks, celebrate effort, and remember:
"The day you least feel like showing up is the day that defines your success."

Step 7: Design Your Success by Design Plan
Fill in the summary below as your personal commitment:
- **My Vision:**

_____

Success by Design: How Smart Entrepreneurs and Creators Build Lasting Habits

- **My Identity Statement:**
  _____

- **My 3 Keystone Habits:**
  _____

- **My System or Routine:**
  _____

- **My Automation Plan:**
  _____

- **My Review Schedule:**
  _____

Signature of Commitment:

I commit to living by design, not by default.
Signature: _____ Date: _____

Connie Ragen Green

Chapter Nine: Revisiting the Precepts That Will Lead You to Your Great Success

"We have tremendous potential for good or ill. How we choose to use that power is up to us; but first we must choose to use it. We're told every day, You can't change the world. But the world is changing every day. Only question is who's doing it? You or somebody else?" ~ J. Michael Straczynski

These five precepts are the philosophical pillars of Success by Design: How Smart Entrepreneurs and Creators Build Lasting Habits.

Each one represents a fundamental truth about what it really takes to achieve long-term success as a marketer, writer, or entrepreneur. Below is an expanded, detailed version of each precept — with both depth and practical insight so that you can include them in the book's early chapters, your workbook companion, or even your live teachings and workshops.

Precept 1: Motivation Is Fleeting; Discipline Is Foundational

Motivation is like a spark — powerful but temporary. It can ignite your enthusiasm, but it won't sustain your fire. Most new entrepreneurs and creators rely too heavily on motivation, waiting for the "right moment" or the "right mood" to take action. But motivation fades. It's tied to emotion, and emotions shift constantly.

Discipline, on the other hand, is steady. It's the engine that keeps moving forward even when the road gets steep. Discipline means honoring your commitments long after the excitement has worn off. It's not about feeling ready — it's about acting regardless of how you feel.

For entrepreneurs, discipline shows up in the mundane: Writing every day, even when ideas don't flow easily.

Posting your content even when engagement feels slow.

Following up with potential clients, even when you'd rather avoid it.

Every act of discipline strengthens your foundation. It builds resilience, reliability, and results. Motivation may get you started, but discipline ensures you arrive at your destination.

Key Lesson: Build your schedule around discipline, not emotion. Let structure carry you when inspiration won't.

Story: The Reluctant Runner – Daniel's Journey

Daniel, a 42-year-old accountant and father of two, always dreamed of running a marathon. He was inspired by motivational YouTube videos and would start running for a few days — then stop as soon as his enthusiasm dipped. Each year, he'd promise himself "this is the one," only to fall off again by the second week.

One evening, after missing yet another training day, Daniel realized that he was chasing motivation instead of building discipline. The next morning, he set a simple rule: put on my running shoes every morning at 6:30 a.m. — no negotiation. He didn't commit to running, just to putting the shoes on.

Over time, that single act became automatic. The shoes led to stepping outside. The short jogs led to longer runs. And six months later, Daniel crossed the finish line of his first marathon — not because he was motivated, but because he was consistent.

His success wasn't fueled by emotion — it was engineered by discipline. Daniel learned that habits are like deposits in a bank account: you don't always see the growth, but the interest compounds over time.

Precept 2: Habits Create Freedom, Not Restriction

Many people view habits as limiting — something that takes away spontaneity. In truth, habits are what give you freedom. When you automate your essential actions, you free your mental energy to focus on creativity, strategy, and innovation.

For entrepreneurs, habits reduce decision fatigue. Instead of asking, "Should I work on my business today?" your habits decide for you. The energy you save by not debating your next step can now be used to elevate your craft or deepen your client relationships.

Well-designed habits create stability and momentum. They anchor your day in intention and give you clarity about what truly matters. This structure is not a cage; it's a framework that supports your growth.

When you have a habit of writing content every morning, your creativity expands.

When you consistently review your business metrics, your confidence in decision-making grows.

When you habitually learn, you evolve faster than the competition.

Key Lesson: Habits are the invisible architecture of freedom. They give you control over your time, your focus, and your results.

Story: The Artist Who Found Time: Marisol's Revelation

Marisol, a 29-year-old painter, believed structure killed creativity. She resisted routines and worked only when "inspired." This led to months of unfinished canvases and constant frustration — she felt guilty for not producing and anxious when she tried to force herself to paint.

After reading about habit systems, she decided to experiment. She set a 60-minute painting block every morning after coffee — even if she didn't feel like painting. The first few days were painful. But soon, she noticed something surprising: her creativity increased.

By painting at the same time daily, her brain started anticipating creativity. She began entering a flow state faster and completing work she once struggled to begin. What felt restrictive became liberating.

Marisol discovered that habits create freedom — freedom from indecision, procrastination, and guilt. The discipline of consistency became the key that unlocked her creativity.

Precept 3: Small Actions, Repeated Consistently, Lead to Massive Results

Success is not built in giant leaps but in deliberate, consistent steps. Every extraordinary achievement you see — a bestselling book, a six-figure launch, a thriving personal brand — is the accumulation of small actions repeated over time.

It's the **compound effect** in motion.

One blog post becomes a library of resources.

One email becomes a list of loyal subscribers.

One video becomes a growing audience.

Consistency magnifies impact. It transforms effort into momentum and momentum into mastery. The results you're chasing are simply the echo of actions you've taken consistently over time.

Many new entrepreneurs give up too soon because they underestimate the power of persistence. They plant seeds but fail to water them long enough to see growth. The truth is that the rewards of consistency are delayed but guaranteed when the actions are aligned with your goals.

Key Lesson: Don't chase intensity; chase consistency. Your future success is being built in the small, unseen moments of today.

Success by Design: How Smart Entrepreneurs and Creators Build Lasting Habits

Story: The Café Transformation – Harold's Habit Shift

At 58, Harold owned a small coffee shop in his town. His business was steady but stagnant. He wanted to attract new customers but didn't know where to start. Instead of making big changes, he decided to improve one small thing every day.

One day, he reorganized the pastry display. The next, he greeted every customer by name. A week later, he added a "Customer of the Week" board. None of these changes felt big. But within six months, his shop became a local favorite — customer reviews soared, and his profits nearly doubled.

When asked what changed, Harold said, "I stopped trying to do everything and started doing something — daily."

Small actions are like drops of water — on their own, they seem insignificant, but over time, they carve stone. Harold's success was not a result of one grand idea, but of 180 small ones stacked over time.

Precept 4: Identity Shapes Behavior—Act Like the Entrepreneur You Want to Become

True transformation begins not with what you do but with who you believe yourself to be. Your identity drives your behavior, and your behavior reinforces your identity — it's a continuous loop.

When you begin to see yourself as a professional, disciplined, successful entrepreneur, your daily choices begin to align with that vision. You naturally act in ways that reflect it — you make time for what matters, you hold yourself accountable, and you operate with confidence instead of hesitation.

This is why surface-level changes rarely last. If your habits conflict with your self-image, your subconscious will always pull you back to what feels "normal." To create lasting success, you must first upgrade your identity.

Ask yourself:

How would the entrepreneur I want to become structure their day?

How would they respond to setbacks?

What habits would they prioritize without fail?

Each small choice to act "as if" reinforces your new identity until it becomes who you truly are.

Key Lesson: Lasting success comes from aligning your habits with your identity. Don't wait to become successful — start behaving like the person who already is.

Story: From Employee to CEO Mindset: Priya's Evolution

Priya, a 35-year-old graphic designer, dreamed of building her own design studio but couldn't seem to leave her corporate job. She saw herself as an "employee" — someone who followed directions and sought approval.

Her mentor once asked her, "How would a CEO make today's decision?" That question became her turning point. Each day, Priya began asking herself, "What would the future me — the successful entrepreneur — do right now?"

When faced with choices — like whether to pitch a new client, update her portfolio, or attend networking events — she made decisions as her future identity. Slowly, she became that person.

Within a year, she launched her design studio and was working with her first five clients. Priya's transformation wasn't about external success — it was an internal shift. She stopped waiting for the right conditions and started embodying her future self before it arrived.

Your identity isn't fixed — it's a choice you renew every day.

Precept 5: Systems Beat Willpower: Structure Your Success

Success by Design: How Smart Entrepreneurs and Creators Build Lasting Habits

Willpower is a limited resource. It's unreliable under stress, fatigue, or distraction. Systems, however, are dependable — they remove the need for constant decision-making and self-control.

A **system** is simply a repeatable process that supports your goals. It's a way to make success automatic by designing your environment, routines, and tools to work in your favor.

For entrepreneurs and creators, effective systems might include:

A weekly content creation plan with built-in deadlines.

A structured marketing workflow that tracks leads and conversions.

A morning routine that primes your focus and energy.

When you rely on systems instead of willpower, you reduce friction and increase follow-through. You stop fighting against yourself and start flowing with a framework that makes success predictable.

Key Lesson: Design your environment and systems to make good choices easy and consistent success inevitable.

Story: The Busy Mompreneur: Evelyn's System

Evelyn, a 47-year-old mother of three, started an online business selling handmade skincare products. At first, she relied entirely on willpower — staying up late to post on social media, answer messages, and fulfill orders. But burnout hit fast.

She felt like she was constantly chasing fires. One evening, she realized she didn't have a business problem — she had a system problem.

Evelyn mapped her week, batching similar tasks together: Mondays were for product creation, Tuesdays for content, Wednesdays for marketing, and Fridays for fulfillment. She automated emails, scheduled posts, and used templates for customer replies.

Within a few weeks, her stress dropped dramatically — and her sales went up.

Evelyn learned that systems don't just make you efficient — they make success sustainable. Willpower fades, but systems persist even on your hardest days.

Closing Reflection

Together, these five precepts form the heart of Success by Design. They remind entrepreneurs and creators that achievement isn't a mystery — it's a method.

You don't need more motivation, inspiration, or luck. You need a structure that supports your discipline, habits that reflect your identity, and systems that make consistency automatic.

That's what this book — and your new way of working — is all about. ~ Connie Ragen Green

Chapter Ten: What's Next for You as You Create Your Own Success by Design?
How to Get From Where You Are Today, to Closer to Exactly Where You Want to Be

"The greater danger for most of us lies not in setting our aim too high and falling short; but in setting our aim too low and achieving our mark." ~ Michelangelo

Introduction: The Moment of Becoming

You've done something powerful — you've completed a journey that most people only think about taking.
Throughout this book, you've explored the principles of habits, discipline, and consistency. You've learned that success isn't an accident — it's *by design.*

But now, we reach the most important turning point of all: what happens next.

This final chapter is your bridge — between learning and living, between knowing and doing. The future you want isn't waiting for permission; it's waiting for *you.*

Quote:
"There comes a moment when you stop planning for the life you want and start *living* it — one deliberate habit at a time."
— *Connie Ragen Green*

Reflect: Where Are You Right Now?

Before you leap forward, take a moment to look around. Success begins with awareness — of what's working, what's not, and who you've become in the process.

Reflection is not regret. It's revelation. It gives you the clarity to see how far you've come and the courage to continue.

Ask Yourself:

What has this book opened my eyes to about success and consistency?

Which habits am I proud of creating — and which ones am I ready to let go of?

How am I already showing up as the person I want to become?

Take a few moments to write your answers below.

Quote:

"Awareness is the seed of transformation. You can't change what you don't recognize."

Decide: What Do You Truly Want Next?

Clarity is your greatest asset. Too many people chase goals that don't belong to them — goals born of comparison, fear, or someone else's expectations.

Your next step must come from *your truth.*

Forget what others think success should look like. Ask yourself instead:

What kind of business do I want to build?

What kind of *life* do I want to live?

How do I want to feel each day as I do my work?

When you make decisions from alignment instead of anxiety, your habits become easier, your actions feel lighter, and your path becomes unmistakably your own.

Your Vision Statement:

"I am creating a life and business that feel aligned with my deepest values and goals."

Write your vision here:

Success by Design: How Smart Entrepreneurs and Creators Build Lasting Habits

Quote:
"Decisions shape destiny — but only when they're rooted in who you truly are." ~ Unknown

Align: Create Your Next-Level Habit Blueprint

Now that you've reflected and decided, it's time to *design*.

Habits are the bridge between your current self and your future self. But not all habits are equal — the ones that matter most are those that create *momentum.*

Here's your three-step **Next-Level Habit Blueprint**:

Choose one keystone habit — something simple yet powerful.

Example: 15 minutes of strategic planning each morning, or daily writing for your blog, book, or marketing content.

Support it with structure.

Systems make discipline easy. Automate, batch, or schedule what matters most.

Track consistency, not perfection.

Progress over perfection — always. Your success is measured by *streaks of effort,* not flawless execution.

Your Keystone Habit:

Supporting System:

Consistency Tracker Start Date:

Quote:
"You don't rise to the level of your goals — you fall to the level of your systems." — *James Clear*

Act: Move Forward with Courage

At some point, all the planning, journaling, and dreaming must turn into one thing — action.

You don't need to have every detail figured out before you begin. You just need the courage to take the first step.

Courage is a muscle, built by movement.

Every small act of consistency rewires your confidence. Every time you keep a promise to yourself, you strengthen your self-trust.

And when self-trust grows, success becomes inevitable.

Action Reflection:

What is one action I will take *today* toward my next goal?

What would I do if I knew I couldn't fail?

Write your answers here:

Quote:

"Confidence doesn't come before action. It's built by it."

Connect: Success Is a Shared Journey

No one builds lasting success alone. Growth happens faster when you surround yourself with people who are walking in the same direction.

Consider joining or forming:

A mastermind group or accountability circle.

A local or online community for entrepreneurs or creators.

A mentorship partnership — both giving and receiving guidance.

Every conversation you have with like-minded people reinforces the truth: you are not alone on this path.

Connection Goals:

Who will I reach out to this week for support or collaboration?

How can I offer value or encouragement to someone else?

Quote:

"Growth shared is growth multiplied."

Your Action Plan: The 7-Day Momentum Challenge

Success by Design: How Smart Entrepreneurs and Creators Build Lasting Habits

Now it's time to *apply everything* you've learned.

For the next seven days, commit to one small, consistent action that aligns with your goals.

Write down your insights and take some time each day to reflect on where you are right now and where you want to be in the near future.

Day	My Action Step	Did I Complete It?	Notes / Wins
Day 1		☐ Yes ☐ No	
Day 2		☐ Yes ☐ No	
Day 3		☐ Yes ☐ No	
Day 4		☐ Yes ☐ No	
Day 5		☐ Yes ☐ No	
Day 6		☐ Yes ☐ No	
Day 7		☐ Yes ☐ No	

Summary/Conclusion
Habits for Success Manifesto: The Precepts That Reshape Your Reality, Redefine Your Identity, and Rebuild Your Future

"I envy the journey you are embarking upon, not because I wish that I was once again at the beginning, but because the world is changing with breakneck speed, giving you the opportunity to serve people all over the world who do not yet know that you are the one that will finally be able to make sense of it all for them." ~ Connie Ragen Green

This supplemental information is intended to inspire, anchor and motivate you, and to set the tone for your great transformation.

I hope that you can now see that your own 'success by design' is closer than you ever thought it could be.

Success is not an accident, a mystery, or a privilege reserved for the lucky.

It is the natural outcome of who you choose to become every single day.

This manifesto is your compass—your reminder that your life shifts when your habits do.

Read it slowly.

Return to it often.

Live it intentionally.

Success isn't about working harder—it's about designing habits that make success inevitable.

Success is the shadow cast by your routines. It follows you when you don't chase it.
When you intentionally build habits that align with your goals, success becomes a by-product—not a battle.
You no longer rely on effort alone; you build a life that pulls you forward.

Success isn't about working harder—it's about designing habits that make success inevitable.

Hard work alone does not guarantee achievement; *alignment* does. When your habits match the goals you claim to want, progress becomes automatic, almost effortless. Most people chase outcomes—they want the book written, the business launched, the health restored. But the wise create *systems* that make those outcomes unavoidable.
Success becomes inevitable when:
Your environment supports the behaviors you want—not the ones you're trying to outgrow.
You eliminate friction and make the right actions the easiest ones to take.
Your habits create momentum, and momentum becomes self-reinforcing.
You design routines that operate even on days you feel tired, stressed, or uninspired.
The truth is, success is never about superhuman effort. It's about establishing rituals that carry you forward even when your energy doesn't.
A well-designed habit is a quiet engine: it hums in the background, compounding results while you live your life.

Success by Design: How Smart Entrepreneurs and Creators Build Lasting Habits

Discipline isn't punishment—it's protection.
It protects your time, your energy, your dreams.
It creates space for inspiration instead of chaos, and it gives you the freedom to focus on what truly matters.
Discipline is not about restriction; it is about liberation.

Discipline isn't a burden; it's a system for freedom and creativity.

People misunderstand discipline—they think it means pressure, rigidity, or punishment. But true discipline is simply *agreement with your future self.*
It is the structure that allows creativity, peace, and flow to flourish.
Without discipline:
You are constantly overwhelmed by decision fatigue.
You waste energy negotiating with yourself all day.
You are enslaved by impulses, distractions, and mood.
With discipline:
You experience clarity, confidence, and ease.
You earn back hours of mental bandwidth.
You create space to innovate, imagine, and rest.
Discipline is not about doing more.
It is about choosing what matters—and choosing it consistently.
It lets you build a life where your time is protected, your boundaries are honored, and your best work can emerge without chaos rushing in to steal it.
Freedom is not the absence of structure.
It is the presence of intentional structure.

Motivation is a spark.
Consistency is the flame.
A structured process—the right routines, the right tools, the right environment—keeps you moving when emotion fades.
You don't wait to feel ready.
You win because you show up anyway.

You don't need more motivation—you need a process that keeps you consistent.

Motivation is unreliable. It is emotional, unstable, easily disrupted by stress, weather, moods, or even a poor night's sleep.

People who succeed at high levels don't depend on motivation—they depend on **systems, sequences, and processes** that keep them steady.

A powerful process does three things:

It removes decision-making.

When a behavior becomes automatic, consistency becomes effortless.

It makes the next step obvious.

Clarity replaces overwhelm, and overwhelm is consistency's greatest enemy.

It creates a rhythm—a predictable pattern you can follow even when the day goes wrong.

The most successful entrepreneurs, writers, creators, and leaders aren't more motivated than you.

They've simply built processes that make failure difficult and consistency natural.

When the process works, you don't have to push yourself— you just follow the path you've already created.

Small, intentional habits create massive, lasting results."

The world celebrates dramatic transformations—overnight successes, monumental wins, breakthrough moments.

But all great success stories share the same hidden truth: they were built on hundreds of tiny decisions that compounded over months and years.

Small habits matter because:

They bypass resistance.

They feel doable, even on your worst days.

They build confidence with every small win.

They create identity shifts— "I am someone who follows through."

They compound like financial interest: slow at first, exponential later.

A 1% improvement repeated daily becomes a 37x improvement in a year.
A five-minute daily action becomes hundreds of hours of progress.
A tiny habit becomes a gateway to a bigger identity.

Small habits generate big results not because they are powerful individually—
but because they are unstoppable collectively.

Progress is not measured in sudden leaps—it is built through steady, deliberate steps.
Five minutes. One action. A single choice.
Small habits compound like interest.
What feels insignificant today becomes unstoppable tomorrow.

What you do daily determines what you achieve permanently.

Your life is shaped not by what you do occasionally, but by what you do consistently.
Daily actions are the architecture of your identity, your business, your relationships, your health, and your future.

Every day you are casting a vote—
for the person you are becoming or the person you are choosing to remain.

Daily habits determine:
Your level of focus
Your emotional resilience
Your productivity
Your creativity
Your sense of purpose
Your financial outcomes
Your sense of self-trust

What you repeat becomes ingrained.
What you ingrain becomes automatic.
What becomes automatic, becomes your life.
If you want a new chapter, change your daily practice.
If you want a new destiny, change your daily decisions.
If you want a new identity, change your daily habits.
Your daily behavior is the most accurate predictor of your long-term success.

What you do daily determines what you achieve permanently.

Your identity is shaped in the quiet moments—when no one is watching, judging, or cheering you on.
Your daily actions reveal your future with remarkable accuracy.
If you want a different outcome, start with a different day.

The Habits for Success Manifesto Promise

I commit to building habits that align with the entrepreneur, creator, or leader I want to become.
I recognize that every small action is a vote for my future.
I understand that consistency, not intensity, transforms my life.
I will design systems that support my success, protect my focus, and fuel my creative energy.
I choose progress over perfection.
I choose identity over impulse.
I choose to become the kind of person who follows through.
Today, I step forward—not with pressure, but with purpose.
Not with overwhelm, but with clarity.
Not with fear, but with intention.
This is the beginning of my next life experience and chapter—one I am fully ready to write.

**Success by Design: How Smart Entrepreneurs and Creators
Build Lasting Habits**

Reading List and Resources

I still remember the day the poster arrived.

It came in one of those long, cardboard tubes that felt far too important to be ordinary mail. The kind you don't open carelessly. The kind that makes your hands move a little slower because something inside feels *special*, even before you know what it is.

The return address said Scholastic Books.

I don't remember ordering it, but I remember knowing immediately that it was meant for me.

When I slid the poster out and carefully unrolled it, there was a sports figure—tall, powerful, mid-motion—someone whose confidence seemed to leap right off the paper. I think it was a basketball player, though the exact face has softened with time. What hasn't faded is the quote printed boldly beneath him:

"Readers are Leaders."

Something about that phrase landed in me differently than anything had before.

Up until that moment, reading had been something I loved quietly. Books were my refuge, my escape, my education when I didn't have one handed to me. But that poster gave reading *meaning*. It gave it power. It suggested that the hours I spent with books weren't just filling time—they were shaping who I could become.

I remember standing there holding that poster, realizing for the first time that the people who changed the world were often the people who read deeply, thought critically, and learned constantly. That leaders weren't just born confident—they were built through curiosity, discipline, and ideas.

And somewhere in that moment, a new thought entered my mind—one I hadn't dared to say out loud yet:

Someday, I want to write a book.

Not because I thought I was special.

Not because I believed it would be easy.

But because I wanted to contribute to the same quiet conversation that had shaped me.

I didn't know when.

I didn't know how.

I didn't even know if it was possible.

But that poster planted a seed.

Years later, after many chapters of my life had been lived the hard way, I would understand something I couldn't yet articulate back then: reading didn't just make me a better student, or a more informed person—it helped me imagine a future I couldn't yet see.

That's why this reading list matters to me.

Every book you read is an invitation to become someone slightly wiser, braver, or more capable than you were before. Every page is a quiet vote for the person you're becoming. And sometimes, one sentence—one quote on a poster—can change the trajectory of your entire life.

Mine did.

And perhaps, somewhere in the pages ahead, one will do the same for you.

The Readers, Leaders, and World Changers Motto

I commit to building habits that align with the entrepreneur, creator, or leader I want to become.

I recognize that every small action is a vote for my future.

I understand that consistency, not intensity, transforms my life.

I will design systems that support my success, protect my focus, and fuel my creative energy.

I choose progress over perfection.

I choose identity over impulse.
I choose to become the kind of person who follows through.

Books I Highly Recommend… and many of these are mentioned throughout this book.

"Drive: The Surprising Truth About What Motivates Us" **by Daniel H. Pink – This book reveals the secret to high performance and satisfaction in all aspects of life, which is the deeply human need to direct our own lives, learn and create new things, and do better by ourselves and our world. Pink also explores intrinsic vs. extrinsic motivation**

"Deep Work: Rules for Focused Success in a Distracted World" **by Cal Newport – This ability to focus without distraction on cognitively demanding tasks—is one of the most important abilities you can cultivate in our current moment. It's a skill that allows you to quickly master complicated information and produce quality results in less time.**

"The Abundance Paradigm: Moving From the Law of Attraction to the Law of Creation" **by Dr. Joe Vitale shows you how to make the profound shift from a paradigm of scarcity in which you have "not enough" of the things you want and need to a paradigm of abundance in which you have more than enough of everything, at all times.**

"The Brain That Changes Itself: Stories of Personal Triumph from the Frontiers of Brain Science" **by Norman Doidge is an immensely moving, inspiring book that will permanently alter the way we look at our brains, human nature, and human potential.**

"Atomic Habits: An Easy & Proven Way to Build Good Habits & Break Bad Ones" **by James Clear reveals practical strategies that will teach you exactly how to form good habits,**

break bad ones, and master the tiny behaviors that lead to remarkable results.

"The Atomic Habits Workbook: Official Companion to the Worldwide Bestseller" (ABOVE) by James Clear. Guided journal prompts will help you engage with your habits and the forces that impact them. Thought-provoking exercises allow you to implement the Atomic Habits theories and see your life transform. This workbook takes the reader from understanding habits to living them.

"The Willpower Instinct: How Self-Control Works, Why It Matters, and What You Can Do to Get More of It" by Kelly McGonigal explains exactly what willpower is, how it works, and why it matters.

"Tiny Habits: The Small Changes that Change Everything" by BJ Fogg will help you increase productivity by tapping into positive emotions to create a happier and healthier life, and how to build behavior without needing motivation.

"Do the Work" by Steven Pressfield is essential reading for understanding resistance and creative discipline. Could you be getting in your way of producing great work? If you've ever started a project but never finished, and would you like to do work that matters, but don't know where to start, you'll learn that it's not about better ideas, it's about pushing through the resistance and actually doing the work.

"Indistractable, Updated Edition: How to Control Your Attention and Choose Your Life" by Nir Eyal reveals the hidden psychology driving us to distraction, and the keys to getting the best out of technology without letting it get the best of us.

"The Compound Effect: Jumpstart Your Income, Your Life, Your Success" by Darren Hardy is based on the principle that

little, everyday decisions will either take you to the life you desire or to disaster by default, and that small, disciplined actions compound into major results over time.

About the Author
Connie Ragen Green Shares Her Life Success Story

My Story — How I Designed a Life I Once Believed Was Out of My Reach
by Connie Ragen Green

People often meet me in person as I am *today* — a confident mentor, bestselling author, and successful online entrepreneur — and assume I must have always been this way.

They see the books, the business, the lifestyle, the calm presence, and think, *"Connie was born for this."* The truth is far more emotional... and far more empowering.

If you're holding this book in your hands, or reading it on your smart phone or computer, or listening to it, there's something you and I already share: a quiet belief — sometimes steady, sometimes fragile — that life can be better than it is right now. I know that belief well. It's been my companion for as long as I can remember, even in the years when it was the only thing I had.

I didn't grow up with certainty or security. I grew up in a world where nothing was promised, where you learned early how to stretch a dollar and how to survive disappointment. I didn't have mentors, or role models, or anyone telling me I was destined for greatness. But I did have a determination I didn't yet know how to name — a whisper that kept saying, *"There's more for you than this."*

I carried that whisper with me through countless jobs — sometimes two or three at a time. I carried it into late-night shifts and early morning responsibilities. I carried it through exhaustion, heartbreak, and days when I wondered whether this was all life would ever be.

What people see now — a bestselling author, an entrepreneur, a mentor — is the tip of the iceberg. What they don't see are the years beneath the surface: the habit-building, the quiet discipline, the countless small actions that moved my life forward in inches long before it moved in miles.

My turning point wasn't dramatic. There was no lightning bolt. One day, at almost fifty years old, I simply told myself the truth:

"I am allowed to reinvent my life."

I left my jobs. Both of them. It wasn't that I didn't love teaching in the classroom and driving hundreds of miles each weekend to complete the real estate appraisals I had been assigned; it was more that I wanted an opportunity to reach a level that had, so far, eluded my grasp. I had dreams to fulfill and people and causes to help make a difference for, and it was time. I stepped into the world of online business with no experience, no guarantees, and no backup plan except grit and curiosity. I made mistakes. So many that I could fill another book — and maybe one day I will. I cried. I learned. I stayed up late figuring out things that most people learn in their twenties. I wrote blog posts no one read at first, created products no one bought at first, and kept going even when quitting would have been easier.

And inch by inch, habit by habit, day by day... everything changed.

I became the person I used to envy — the person who was consistent, confident, and courageous. Not because I woke up motivated, but because I built habits that made success *inevitable*.

That's what this book is really about.

Not willpower.

Not talent.

Not luck.

Habits. Discipline. Consistency.

The three things that rebuilt my life from the inside out.

I wrote this book because I know what it feels like to start over. I know what it feels like to be overwhelmed, to doubt yourself, to fear that maybe you missed your chance. I also know — with absolute certainty — that your life can change dramatically through small, deliberate habits practiced with intention.

I've lived the "iceberg illusion."
People see the success, but not the years of work beneath it — the late nights, the tiny steps, the personal reinvention.
This book reveals that beneath-the-surface truth.

Today, my deepest mission is simple:
To help you design a life that feels like freedom — one habit, one day, one brave decision at a time.

If I could change everything starting at forty — after decades of struggling, doubting, and wondering if I'd ever break through — then trust me... you can, too.

And if this book becomes even a small part of your transformation, then every step of my journey — every mistake, every tear, every late-night moment of doubt — was worth it.

Let's design your success story next.
I'm cheering for you already.
— Connie Ragen Green

www.ingramcontent.com/pod-product-compliance
Lightning Source LLC
Chambersburg PA
CBHW070931210326
41520CB00021B/6888